RECEIVED

SEP 18 2019

BROADVIEW LIBRARY

NO LONGER PROPERTY OF
SEATTLE PUBLIC LIBRARY

Bring Your Brain to Work

Bring Your Brain to Work

*Using Cognitive Science to
Get a Job, Do It Well, and
Advance Your Career*

ART MARKMAN

Harvard Business Review Press

Boston, Massachusetts

HBR Press Quantity Sales Discounts

Harvard Business Review Press titles are available at significant quantity discounts when purchased in bulk for client gifts, sales promotions, and premiums. Special editions, including books with corporate logos, customized covers, and letters from the company or CEO printed in the front matter, as well as excerpts of existing books, can also be created in large quantities for special needs.

For details and discount information for both print and
ebook formats, contact booksales@harvardbusiness.org,
tel. 800-988-0886, or www.hbr.org/bulksales.

Copyright 2019 Art Markman
All rights reserved
Printed in the United States of America

10 9 8 7 6 5 4 3 2 1

No part of this publication may be reproduced, stored in or introduced into a retrieval system, or transmitted, in any form, or by any means (electronic, mechanical, photocopying, recording, or otherwise), without the prior permission of the publisher. Requests for permission should be directed to permissions@hbsp.harvard.edu, or mailed to Permissions, Harvard Business School Publishing, 60 Harvard Way, Boston, Massachusetts 02163.

The web addresses referenced in this book were live and correct at the time of the book's publication but may be subject to change.

Library of Congress Cataloging-in-Publication Data

Names: Markman, Arthur B., author.
Title: Bring your brain to work / Art Markman (PhD.)
Description: Boston, Massachusetts : Harvard Business Review Press, [2019] |
   Includes bibliographical references.
Identifiers: LCCN 2018060284 | ISBN 9781633696112 (hardcover)
Subjects: LCSH: Vocational guidance. | Psychology, Industrial. | Success in
   business. | Cognitive science.
Classification: LCC HF5381 .M268 2019 | DDC 158.7—dc23
LC record available at https://lccn.loc.gov/2018060284
   ISBN: 978-1-63369-611-2
   eISBN: 978-1-63369-612-9

The paper used in this publication meets the requirements of the American National Standard for Permanence of Paper for Publications and Documents in Libraries and Archives Z39.48-1992.

To Amy, Lewis, Lauren, Jessica, Rolee, and

Alyx for making HDO what it is today

CONTENTS

PART THREE

Managing Your Career

Bring Your Brain to Work

1

The Path to Success Runs through Cognitive Science

I f you're like most people, your formal education served many functions. You may have learned technical skills to prepare you for a particular career. You may have been given a chance to develop broad critical thinking. Perhaps you focused on your communication abilities. But your education did not prepare you for your career—at least not entirely—because so many factors determine how well things go for you at work.

As a college professor, I spend a lot of time around people who are thinking about their careers. Undergrads worry about getting a first job after college. Graduate students are often deciding between an academic career and work in industry, government, or nonprofits. I helped create the master's program in Human Dimensions of Organizations, which teaches mid-career professionals about people. The students use the program as a means of career advancement—some to transition from one career to another, and others to enhance the work they already do.

Over time, I realized that a lot of psychology research is relevant to the way people think about their careers, but few people have been exposed to it. I was thinking about that while on the phone with my oldest son, who was twenty-three at the time. He was describing a difficult day he'd had at work. Someone in the office had yelled at him for revealing a piece of information to a client that the angry colleague didn't think ought to have been said.

What should my son do in that situation? Go to his boss and tell her what happened? Try to remedy the situation with the client? Have a conversation with the offended colleague? How could he even begin to figure out what he did wrong and how to fix it? What would you do in this situation? Take a moment to think about it.

Now ask yourself, What class did I take to learn how to deal with a work situation like this one? You probably can't think of one.

The need for such lessons doesn't end after your first job. Suppose you were the supervisor of a young employee who'd just been yelled at by a colleague. How would you handle the situation? Would you punish the new employee for divulging the information? Would you get angry at the colleague for yelling? Would you try to get the two of them to handle this tiff themselves? Is there another alternative?

So much of what happens in your work life, starting with when you look for your first job, falls outside what you spent the first two decades of your life learning. College students may hear about careers that follow from their major, but they don't learn much about how to actually get that first job. Writing classes focus on how to create well-crafted paragraphs, but not on how to talk to an irate colleague or to motivate coworkers to rally around a project. Studying for exams helps you correct mistakes in material you are learning, but it doesn't tell you how to fix problems with a project that is about to be delivered to a client. In the education system, your progress is mapped out from grade to grade and from class to class. But how do you know when it's time to move on to the next job, or even what steps to take to turn a collection of jobs into a career?

Many people manage to muddle through these situations. They make some mistakes and (one hopes) learn from them. They impress some colleagues and make mortal enemies of others. And when they look back on their years of work, they can tell a story about the factors that (they believe) led to their success.

Some of these people even go on to write books about how to succeed at work and be a leader in the workplace. They elevate the philosophy underlying their particular career choices to the level of advice that everyone should follow. Unfortunately, it's hard to separate out the truly crucial choices people made from the many other factors (which we sometimes call luck or chance) that affected their paths. It would be much better to draw advice from looking across the experiences of many people.

That is where cognitive science—the study of minds and brains—comes in. Cognitive science includes psychology, neuroscience, anthropology, computer science, and philosophy. As a thriving area of research, it has a lot to say about the way people think, feel, and act that has practical implications for how you should live your life—particularly at work.

This research says a lot about how to motivate yourself to get work done, to learn the new skills that are required for your job, and to deal with your colleagues, clients, and customers. It can explain why you work the way you do. It can also suggest strategies to help you avoid blind alleys at work and recover faster from your mistakes.

So, let's get started.

Making the Most of Your Career

A big problem with the word *success* is that it's a noun.

When you say someone is a success, you're placing them in the category of successful people. Psychologists have found that when you categorize someone like this, you assume that they have some *essence* that makes them belong in that category. This may make sense for some categories, such as animals. It's reasonable to assume that something is a cat if it has some essence of cat—cat DNA, for example. It makes less sense when applied to people, but we still do it. We assume that Fran is a painter not just because she paints, but because she has some deep quality that makes her fit that category. Jesse is anxious because he has some quality that makes him an anxious person.

Likewise, when you think of someone as a success, you assume that they have an essential quality that makes them successful. You may worry that you don't have that quality, and thus that you may not be able to excel.

If you leave behind the noun and move to a verb—*succeed*—everything changes.

The primary function of verbs is to refer to actions. Success is a series of actions that culminate in achieving desired outcomes. It requires continual effort to improve. It involves growth that supports the transition from one position to another across the length of a career. Success demands the motivation to excel over a long time span. The same is true for other categories, such as *leader* and *innovator*. There are a few qualities that help someone succeed, lead, or innovate, but it is the process of working, rather than the qualities of the individual, that creates the most desirable outcomes.

The idea that you have to put in effort to develop a career is not news. That said, many people put their effort into the wrong activities. They worry about things that are out of their control, but fail to act on things that they can influence. They neglect crucial tasks that lead to good outcomes.

This book aims to help you understand how to develop your career using cognitive science. To do this effectively, you need to do two things. First, you must appreciate the three phases that define a career path: getting a job, excelling, and moving on. Second, you should become acquainted with the three brain systems that will help you achieve your goals: the motivational brain, the social brain, and the cognitive brain.

The Career Cycle

What exactly is a career? Ask around, and some consensus emerges. Careers are bigger than particular jobs. They involve building a skill set that enables you to contribute to an organization, an industry, or a field. Not every job someone holds is part of their career. A premed college student who works as a short-order cook while in school is not developing a career. A budding chef who spends three years as a line cook is doing a similar job, but is developing career-level experience.

Although people can often identify the threads of their careers, it's actually quite difficult to precisely define what a career entails. In fact, the Bureau of Labor Statistics keeps track of the number of jobs people have over a lifetime, but not the number of careers.

Part of the problem in defining your career is that often it becomes clear only when you look back over your life. As you are moving forward, living your life, it may not be obvious that you have switched careers.

For example, after going to graduate school in psychology at the University of Illinois, I was a faculty member at Northwestern University, at Columbia University, and finally at the University of Texas, where I am today. From this standpoint, it might seem that I had three jobs, but one career—as a professor.

Yet there are other ways of looking at this same situation. From the start of graduate school until about my tenth year at the University of Texas, my primary focus was on doing basic research for publication in academic journals. Starting in my tenth year, I began trying to communicate research in my field to a broader public, through blogs, books (like this one), and a radio show called *Two Guys on Your Head.*

I also did outreach to companies that wanted to learn more about cognitive science and to use it in their businesses and began consulting for them. So is this a second career or part of the first one? Is the external communication part of the same aspect of my career as the consulting, or are they separate?

To complicate the story further, in my twelfth year at UT, I became the director of the Human Dimensions of Organizations program, which teaches undergraduates and master's students about the people they encounter in the workplace. Is this administrative role part of my teaching career? Part of my communication/consulting career? Separate from both? They all feel like some part of my career trajectory—certainly more so than the time I spend as a saxophone player in a ska band. For example, without having spent time consulting for companies, I would have had difficulty running a master's program aimed at working professionals.

Because it's so hard to define a career, I'll focus primarily on jobs and positions in this book, although in chapter 10 I return to the idea of managing a career rather than just thinking about particular jobs.

A *job* is somewhat easier to define. The Bureau of Labor Statistics deems it an uninterrupted period of work for a particular employer. A *position* is a role that someone takes on for an employer. A person may hold many positions within an organization over a number of years, but a period of working for the same employer consists of one job.

A survey by the Bureau of Labor Statistics released in 2015 looked at a subset of Baby Boomers born from 1957 to 1964. These people held an average of 11.7 jobs between the ages of eighteen and forty-eight. That means that the people in this survey changed jobs, on average, every two to three years over the first thirty years they were in the workforce. That's a lot of movement. If anything, this trend is accelerating.

The job cycle has three phases: seeking a job, doing the job, and moving on. These phases are not always completely separate. You might seek another position (with the same company or another one) while you're working. You might choose to get education for a career change without leaving your current job. But they are separate enough that it's worth treating them independently.

Most people recognize the three phases of the job cycle, but they may be unfamiliar with specific aspects of them. Ask yourself which of the following things you're sure you already know.

- The process recruiters go through to evaluate applications.

- The best way to communicate what you don't know in a job interview.

- What you learn about a potential employer from the interview.

- How to recover from a big mistake at work.

- How to deal with a supervisor who seems not to have your best interests at heart.

- Why your workplace is stressful and what to do about it.

- Whether you should compare your performance with that of your colleagues.

- How to deal with becoming a supervisor of your friends.

- What causes dissatisfaction with your job.

- What to tell your current employer about applying for a new job.

- When it's time to think about getting another degree.

One item on this list came out of a conversation I had with a participant in a seminar I taught. She had worked for several years at a medium-size tech company that strives for a collegial work environment. She entered the organization with eight other people about her age, and the group bonded over long work hours and drinks after work. When I met her, she had been put on a fast track for promotion to supervisor.

After the promotion, some of her friends would be her direct reports, and she was struggling with the implications. Over drinks, her friends often complained about managers. Now she was about to go from being one of "us" to being one of "them." Some of the reason for her stress was obvious—she worried about the prospect of having to give a negative evaluation to a friend. But—somewhat less obviously—she couldn't decide whether she should still go to happy hour with her cohort.

As this example demonstrates, the specific situations you face at work bring up all kinds of issues that can be hard to envision and to prepare for. But plenty of research exists that can help you manage your positions, your jobs, and your career cycle as a whole.

First you need to understand your own brain.

Your Brain(s)

President George H. W. Bush named the decade 1990–1999 "The Decade of the Brain" to motivate continued investment in our understanding of that wondrous organ. Fascination with the human brain has only grown since then. Evidence exists that people believe more strongly in findings from psychology if the research includes some discussion of how the brain brought about those results. More recently, using the prefix "neuro-" has become a surefire way to generate excitement about a field (or at least to pump up interest from the market). Specialists now exist in neuroeconomics and neuromarketing, for example.

I'm guilty of taking advantage of this interest in the way I've written this book. My field of specialty is cognitive science—the interdisciplinary field I mentioned earlier in this chapter. I've done most of my research using the methods of psychology, though I have ventured into many of the other disciplines of cognitive science, including neuroscience, over the course of my career.

That said, most of what I'm going to present comes out of the field of psychology. Often, when we use the language of psychology and talk about concepts such as memory, attention, motivation, and language, we are talking about the *mind*. Those concepts are implemented by the human brain just as the programming concepts underlying word processors and web browsers are implemented by the particular hardware you use.

On a few occasions, I will dip down to the level of neuroscience to talk about a key feature of the brain that's important for understanding the mind. But science has learned little about brain function that suggests different ways we should engage complex aspects of thinking such as understanding how to work more effectively or how to market products to people. Anyone who attempts to persuade you otherwise is really selling you psychology by dressing it up in language they hope you'll find more "scientific."

In this book, I focus on three important mental systems that are crucial for success at work: the *motivational* brain, the *social* brain, and the *cognitive* brain. I'm using these terms loosely. You don't really have three separate brains. In fact, the parts of the brain that serve motivational, social, and cognitive functions are physiologically intertwined. But these aspects of the way the mind/brain works are often studied independently and explained with different theories. So I find it valuable to give them different names. And by treating them separately, I can help you understand how to apply the suggestions in this book to your work.

Your motivational brain is the set of mechanisms that get you to do something (or sometimes avoid doing something). The core brain regions that are part of the motivational brain are evolutionarily very old. They are the areas you would also find in the brains of rats, mice, and deer—creatures from which the human branch of evolution split off a long time ago. Knowing what motivates you, your colleagues, and your supervisors is important for managing your own work and for understanding the sources of stress and satisfaction in the tasks you do.

Your social brain is the collection of systems that help you deal with other people. Much of your education through college is an individual sport, but work is most often a team sport. You have to recognize how people will evaluate you. You have to devote effort to getting groups to work together to achieve collective goals. You have to do a good job of predicting how other people will react in order to achieve your goals and to help them achieve theirs. The human brain evolved to help you work with others. After all, humans dominate the planet because of our ability to coordinate activity, not because of our fearsome physical prowess. The social brain is what that participant in my seminar needed to use to deal with becoming a supervisor. I'll take up her story again in chapter 8.

Your cognitive brain is the elaborate set of structures that permit you to communicate, make excellent snap judgments on the basis of your experience, and engage in complex reasoning. You've probably heard the cliché that in business it's not what you know that matters, it's who you know. Who you know matters a lot. But if you don't actually know a lot, people are likely to think you're incompetent. It's probably better to say that both what you know and who you know allow you to succeed.

Over the course of this book, I'll introduce you to a lot of details about your brain(s). Sometimes I'll call out these brains by name, sometimes not. What is most important is that you have to draw on motivational, social, and cognitive factors to succeed over the course of your career. The more you learn about how you think, the easier it will be to work in a way that fits naturally with how your brain wants to function.

BONUS BRAIN:

The Jazz Brain

Another remarkable facet of humans is our capacity to improvise. People are very good at dealing with new situations and at revising a plan on the fly. To do those things well, though, it's important to understand the core elements of improvisation. In several chapters, I'll present information about how to improvise in boxes like this one. I should say at the outset that musically, I was born a generation or two later than I should have been. Rather than the '80s New Wave and synthpop I grew up with, I've always gravitated to jazz; I even took up the saxophone in my thirties just to learn more about the music. I never realized that my hobby would feed back into my professional life.

Good improvisation requires expertise. It's natural to assume that people with extensive experience become imprisoned by it and so are unable to see situations in a new way. That can certainly happen. But an unwillingness to consider new opportunities or new ways of doing things doesn't result from experience.

Indeed, the most flexible individuals are those with considerable knowledge in a domain. Experts are best able to recall things from the past that may be useful for adapting to new circumstances. They can also imagine the outcome of a particular course of action, so they can judge well whether that action is likely to succeed.

For this reason, it's important to expose yourself to many different situations in the workplace. It can be uncomfortable to do something unfamiliar, and the first time you try, you're likely to make plenty of mistakes. But the wider the range of things you have done, the more flexibly you'll be able to work in the future.

The Plan

This book brings together research on your brain with the kinds of situations you may encounter across the three stages of the job cycle.

Getting a job, excelling at it, and moving on to a new one all involve your motivational, social, and cognitive brains.

If you've picked up this book, chances are good that you're primarily concerned with one of the three stages of the job cycle. If so, feel free to start reading in the section most pertinent to your current goals. The sections and chapters are written to be as self-contained as possible. I point forward and back to related material as well, in case you started in the middle. That said, you never know when you might find a nugget that is useful to you now from a section focused primarily on another stage of your career.

You might also be wondering whether this book is for you. If you're fairly new to the workplace, a lot of what I discuss here will probably be unfamiliar. Even if you are in the middle of your career, you may have developed ideas about how to manage your work life without thinking about the psychology underlying it. If you're already embedded in your career, you might want to focus on part 2 first and explore ways to improve your performance at work. Finally, even if you're not actively searching for a job or even looking to move to a new position, you'll probably have to give advice to colleagues, friends, and mentees who are. This book will give you a vocabulary for talking with others about how to manage their work life.

You should know up front that this is going to take some effort on your part. You spent years in school developing the expertise that would help you get your first job. You're going to have to put in some time to optimize your motivational, social, and cognitive brains to develop your career. Someday, perhaps, we'll be able to upload all those skills the way Neo learned kung fu in *The Matrix*.

But for now, my aim is to help you understand the functioning of your brain (and the brains of your colleagues, clients, and customers). I want you to have enough knowledge to make effective decisions about complicated work situations. I'll illustrate these principles with stories drawn from interviews and gathered from contacts on social media. There is no one-size-fits-all answer to complicated problems. The better able you are to bring your brain to work, the more options you give yourself for solving difficult problems.

Throughout this book, I base my recommendations on studies and conclusions drawn from the literature in psychology. At times, I'll name a particular researcher or study in the text. Sometimes, to keep things conversational, I won't provide much more information in the text itself. At the end of the book, though, my sources are listed by chapter.

I also try to illustrate key points with stories about people at different stages of their careers. Unless I note otherwise, these stories were sent to me by people in my social media network who volunteered information about their experiences in response to one of many inquiries I made as I was writing the book. They are identified by first name only, and some details have been omitted to protect their anonymity.

Each of the following chapters ends with two lists of takeaways. One focuses on the core cognitive science concepts in the chapter, the other on specific tips. You can use these sections to find things you want to revisit.

To return to my opening anecdote: My son went back to his desk and spent some time thinking about what he had done that led his colleague to yell at him. Then he approached his boss and explained the situation. He apologized for what he had told the client and gave his best idea for what he might have done differently. Then he asked his boss for advice about how to deal with such a situation better should it happen again.

Was that the right thing for him to do?

Read on.

PART ONE

Getting a Job

2

Finding Opportunities You'll Value

I love the University of Texas in many ways. It's an excellent and supportive place to be a professor. The undergraduate and graduate students are excellent. The facilities are top-notch. The school fosters a healthful work environment.

But one thing really bugs me. We ask our undergrads to pick a major before they arrive on campus. A few hold out and select something soon after arriving, but the longer they wait, the harder it is for them to graduate in four years. It's particularly difficult if a student wants to transfer across units within the university—say, from liberal arts to natural sciences, or from communications to business.

The problem is that most people at eighteen have no idea what they want to do with their lives. Five-year-olds want to be astronauts, dancers, race-car drivers, and chefs. The imagination of eighteen-year-olds is limited by what they have been exposed to so far. They know the jobs they've seen their parents and other nearby adults doing. Their K–12 education was typically focused on a narrow range of subjects. My own experience was certainly like that. When I was a senior in high school, I took a survey of career interests that recommended I consider a career in accounting. I'm pretty sure that reflected the fact that my father is an accountant rather than that I had any particular interest in the field.

I believe it's important for students to spend some time exploring a range of topics to get a sense of what subjects are interesting to them. There's no good reason to stick with the interests you have at eighteen (or twenty-five, or forty, for that matter). The workplace is constantly changing. New job opportunities and career paths are opening all the time as a result of technology. In addition, changes in the marketplace have made some jobs obsolete.

Even people who have been working for many years may find that they're ready to make a significant change. I will talk about signs that you need to move on in chapter 9. Once you make that decision, though, the process of finding a new job is pretty similar to what you would have to do if you were just starting out. And many of the same issues apply.

Should You Find Your Passion?

One of the more overused phrases tossed out at college students and job-seekers is "Find your passion." The advice is well-meaning. People who are excited about their careers will put in long hours and overcome obstacles to reach a goal. They have a feeling of satisfaction about their work and are more resilient to setbacks. So the assumption is that when people find something they are passionate about, it naturally leads to such commitment.

Before evaluating this idea, let's dig into the motivational brain. Where does passion come from?

Your feelings emerge from the motivational brain. Many of its circuits involve the basal ganglia, which are structures deep inside the organ. As I mentioned in chapter 1, these structures are similar to those in other animals, such as rats, mice, and deer. Where the human brain differs from those of other animals is in the size of the cortex—the outer surface.

The regions deep in the brain don't have extensive connections to the areas of the cortex that control the social and cognitive brains. As a result, people have little ability to introspect about what drives their motivational system. Instead, the motivational brain communicates with the cognitive and social brains largely through feelings.

The feelings you have (what psychologists call *affect*) are actually rather simple. When you're making progress toward achieving your goals, you feel good. When you aren't, you feel bad. The more deeply invested you are in the goal the motivational system is pursuing, the stronger the feelings you have.

These feelings become emotions when you reflect on them. You don't consciously realize what factors are driving your motivational system to produce your affect. You experience a particular emotion only after giving your own interpretation to those feelings.

Passion arises from strong positive feelings. When you believe that the object of those feelings is your job and your work—when you are deeply invested in what you're doing and you believe that you're making progress toward your goals—you experience excitement, joy, satisfaction, and passion for your work.

What do we know about the factors that lead people to the kind of motivational engagement that we call passion?

Many things can lead you to be happy at work, and they will emerge throughout this book. For now, though, I'm going to focus on passion. What makes people truly excited about the work they do?

Quite a bit of research provides evidence for the importance of seeing work not just as a job but as a *calling* or a *vocation*. Bryan Dik and Ryan Duffy suggest that a vocation involves focusing on any task (work, parenting, social action) as something that gives a sense of meaning or purpose to life, particularly if the goal is to help others rather than the self. Jane Dawson reviews the use of the word *vocation* to refer to work and points out that the German sociologist Max Weber thought it would benefit people to see their work as something connected with selfless service to others. Contemporary research suggests that people who view what they do as a calling commit more strongly to their work than do people who view it as just a job or a means to make a living.

You may think that seeing work as a calling requires doing particular tasks that seem truly important on the surface—that someone sorting packages in the mailroom or cleaning toilets is unlikely to imbue those tasks with meaning, whereas someone who is leading an organization, doing research on a disease, or saving animals in a shelter should find it easy to see the work as meaningful.

But as it turns out, people have a remarkable capacity to define what they're doing in a variety of ways. A story is told about President Kennedy on a visit to Cape Canaveral, talking to a maintenance worker and asking him, "What are you doing here?" The man replied, "Sending a man to the moon." Although this story is probably apocryphal, people often clearly view the specific tasks they perform as serving a larger mission—even when the tasks don't seem very interesting.

Of course, the more directly connected your work seems to a broader societal outcome, the easier it is to view your job as having significance. And believing in the mission of the organization you work for enhances the sense that your work is important. As an example, I had the opportunity to speak to staff members from Hospice Austin, an organization that provides end-of-life care to patients with terminal illnesses. No matter what role they play in that organization—from manager to social worker to care professional—they all feel that they are doing something of immense importance. The job can be difficult, and people often need a break from the emotional toll, but they all recognize that they are making an important contribution to their community.

That said, there are big differences in what people find important. I have met employees of Procter & Gamble who were excited about their work on toilet paper, and others at the same company who found it hard to generate enthusiasm for the next round of innovation on toothpaste. I've met people who leaped out of bed each day eager for the chance to win new accounts in business-to-business marketing, and others who viewed their work influencing the behavior of consumers with deep cynicism. I love my job as an academic, but I've had colleagues over the years who were burned out and disengaged.

So where does this passion for work come from?

There are two possibilities. One is that everybody has a relatively fixed set of interests, and someone's initial reaction to a job is a good predictor of that person's long-term love for the work. A second possibility is that people can learn to love almost any job.

The advice to find your passion clearly assumes the first of these possibilities. You either love something or you don't, and if you're not excited about the work you're doing, you should seriously think about moving on.

The reality is more complicated. Research by Patricia Chen, Phoebe Ellsworth, and Norbert Schwarz finds that some people believe their passions are fixed. As a result, they make fast judgments about whether they like a particular profession. They are prone to leave jobs quickly and to change jobs often early in their careers until they find something they really enjoy. Other people believe they can learn to love almost any career. These individuals stick longer with their early jobs. Interestingly, both types of people are about equally happy with their careers in the long term.

What does this mean for you?

Much depends on how willing you are to learn to love the work you're doing, and how much tolerance you have for switching jobs. It appears that people can learn to love almost any career path if they are open to it. But if you're willing to change jobs and start over a few times, you might be able to find a career path that is more love at first sight than acquired taste.

I once talked about this issue with Pete Foley, who spent many years working for Procter & Gamble. He pointed out that most jobs are multifaceted, so you can "evolve them into something you love, at least most of the time . . . very few jobs remain static, so [you can] actively nudge your role in a direction you love." The key insight here is that the tasks that characterize your work initially need not be the ones that define your job over the long term. If you believe in the mission of the organization you work for, you can often find ways to achieve that mission by doing specific aspects of your job that also bring you satisfaction.

This understanding of where passion comes from is important because people often find their job choices constrained by factors beyond their control. I have met people who followed a partner across the country and then had to find a job in their own field in that location. I've known individuals who had to work particular hours of the day in order to care for an ailing relative. In cases like these, it's easy to become frustrated about job prospects. When you have the freedom to take a job anywhere, you can follow your passion wherever it leads. If other factors limit you, the job you take may not be the one you dreamed of.

If you are under such constraints, you may resent the people or circumstances that prevented you from following an exciting job prospect. It's easy to feel boxed in by these situations. One way to seize control over your circumstances, though, is to decide how you want to react to the job you take. If you choose to focus on the ways the job can help society more broadly, and on how the impact of the job is bigger than the tasks you're asked to perform, you can take a step toward seeing that job as a calling.

Consideration Sets and Values

Finding a job is generally not like buying a blender. If you discover you need a blender, as I did one Sunday morning a few years ago, you hop in the car and make your way to a big-box retailer (often armed with a coupon for 20 percent off) and stand in front of the wall of blenders hoping to find one that suits your needs at a reasonable price. The collection of blenders you have to choose from (what decision scientists call a *consideration set*) is determined by the store you choose.

In some professions, jobs are like that. Before I got my first academic position, I went to two trade publications—the *APA Monitor* and the *APS Observer*. Every psychology department in the country posts its fall job openings in one (or both) of those publications, which are maintained by the two dominant professional societies for psychologists. If you're looking for a job as an assistant professor, you scour the ads and send off your application materials to each possibility, hoping to get an interview.

Most of the time, though, picking your consideration set is nothing like that. Instead, you have to do a lot of problem solving. That's where your cognitive brain comes in.

The first problem you have to solve is deciding what jobs to apply for. That requires being explicit about the values that are most important to you. Aligning your job with your values is important, because although you can learn to love the particular things you do for a job, it's hard to stay motivated when the organization's mission is inconsistent with what you value.

It takes time for some people to figure out what their core values are. You develop your values in part from the broader culture around you, in part from your experiences, and in part from spending time thinking about what you want. You internalize cultural values from conversations with other people, from depictions of careers in the media, and from your education. High school places an emphasis on going to college. Majors in college emphasize specific career paths and promote values related to them.

But you can take the time to determine what your values are and then find jobs that match them. Along the way, you'll recognize that the major you selected in college helped you hone many problem-solving, thinking, and communication skills above and beyond the content that defined the discipline you studied.

For example, Bryan left college and focused on applying for jobs that had titles he felt would command respect from relatives, friends, and people in the workplace. He also focused on potential careers that would pay well. After taking his first job, he discovered that the day-to-day work was mind-numbing, and at the age of twenty-five he joined the Peace Corps, which gave him a more global perspective. Through that experience he realized that he was going to get his satisfaction not from the appearance of a job but, rather, from helping people develop their own potential.

In another example, Jason was profoundly affected by the loss of his brother. This tragedy forced him to think about what he wanted to accomplish in life and to ask the question "If [I] were to die today or in two weeks, would [I] be happy with [my] contribution?" He tried out several jobs to help him understand how best to help other people, and ultimately focused on a career in marketing to find ways of influencing people to engage in behaviors they already know are good for them.

Stories about people's search for their values have a few commonalities. First, people are often unaware of the values they've adopted from the culture around them until they notice a mismatch between the actions they've pursued and their reactions. Bryan looked for jobs that focused on values he had adopted from the broader culture—power and achievement—and then (to his surprise) discovered that he was not enjoying the work. That led him to question whether he truly understood his own values, which ultimately led him to the Peace Corps, where he pursued values of benevolence and universalism. I'll talk more about the kinds of values people hold in the next section.

Second, many people revisit their core values after an extreme experience such as the death of a loved one. Jason used the death of his brother to engage in mental time travel. He projected himself to the end of his life and imagined looking back on it, wondering whether he would be happy with what he had accomplished. This response fits with the work of Tom Gilovich and Victoria Medvec, who found that older adults tend to regret things they haven't done because they won't have the opportunity to engage in those activities. When you imagine yourself at the end of your life, it tends to focus you on things you haven't yet accomplished.

Even without an event that reminds you of your mortality, it's useful to think about what you may regret not having done. Every year or so, ask yourself whether there is something you hope to accomplish in your life that you haven't made progress on. If so, it might be worth devoting some of your time toward it. When your potential regrets include career goals, you should think about ways to realign your career path.

Third, there is a tendency for people's values to shift over time as a result of both changes in beliefs and changes in life stage. For example, one member of my community was a successful attorney for several decades. Early on, he focused on advancing and making partner in his firm. When his children were young, he backed off from work to help raise his family, particularly when his wife had some health problems. After the kids grew up, he recommitted to his career in law for a while. As he approached retirement, though, he decided to leave the practice of law and run a nonprofit. His children were grown and his house was paid for, so he opted to focus his energies on helping his community. Each of these decisions about managing his career reflected changes in which values were central to his life. I will return to the issue of shifting values in chapter 9.

Exploring Your Values

Values are general motivations that guide people's actions over the long term. That is, your motivational brain lies at the heart of your values. These values are abstract long-term policies, though people can change their values over time. Shalom Schwartz has devoted his research career to exploring the overarching set of values that people hold. His research suggests that the culture to which people belong has a profound influence on the values they adopt. Different cultures promote different values. Figure 2-1 shows the wheel of values that emerged from Schwartz's work. This framework suggests that ten universal values exist.

FIGURE 2-1

Ten universal values

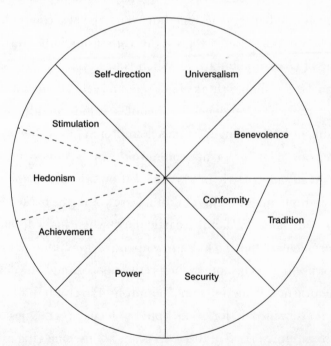

Source: Republished with permission of SAGE Publications, from "Values and Behaviors: Strengths and Structure of Relations," Anat Bardi and Shalom Schwartz, *Personality and Social Psychology Bulletin 29*, no. 10 (2003); permission conveyed through Copyright Clearance Center, Inc.

TABLE 2-1

Value definitions

Power: Control over people and resources, social status

Achievement: Personal success (as defined by social standards)

Hedonism: Pleasure, enjoyment, and self-gratification

Stimulation: Excitement, pursuit of novelty and challenge

Self-direction: Independence in thought and action; creativity

Universalism: Tolerance, appreciation, and acceptance of all people and nature

Benevolence: Helping others and protecting their welfare

Conformity: Restraining actions and impulses to fit social norms

Tradition: Respect for cultural customs, norms, and ideas

Security: Safety and stability in self, society, and relationships

In this wheel, neighboring values are similar to each other, while those across the wheel are contradictory. Power and achievement, which Bryan adopted at first, are similar, as are universalism and benevolence—almost across the wheel—to which he shifted to after joining the Peace Corps. Table 2-1 gives a brief definition of the values in this system.

You can clarify your own values in two ways. First, just by reading over this list, you may find that some values, but not others, resonate with you. Take note of which ones you feel best describe you.

Surveys that ask you questions about your values can also be illuminating. Chris told me that he went to an information session where overseas jobs with the US government were described. As part of the process, attendees took a survey; later, at lunch, several potential applicants compared their responses. Several of them laughed at the item "I would like to work in a war zone" and wondered who would strongly agree with that. That was when Chris—who was excited about the prospect of working in a war zone—realized that his values were not necessarily like everyone else's. He clearly desired stimulation more than did some other people in the group. He ended up overseas in some dangerous places—and he enjoyed it immensely.

Second, observe the reactions you have to your own actions and those of other people. When you do something and enjoy it, make a note. When someone else does something you don't like or are uncomfortable with, note that as well. Now explain to yourself why you did or didn't like that action. Your explanation will probably refer to the values you hold.

Better still, engage your social brain in this process. Find someone who can serve as a sounding board for you without telling you what to do. Talk through what you want and why. The advantage of talking to someone else over just thinking about it yourself is that you have to articulate a number of hidden assumptions. You may only think you understand why you feel the way you do about a job or a career path. When you describe it to someone else, you have to unpack the reasons for your feelings and find a vocabulary for talking about them. That will often give you more insight into your values than just introspecting about them.

It may seem obvious that your values determine your judgments of what is good or bad. After all, the word *evaluate* even has *value* buried in it. But when you start watching your own reactions carefully, you may discover a disconnect between what you thought you valued and what is actually important to you. Bryan believed that he wanted a career that would lead to achievement. But when he looked more carefully at the activities and outcomes he truly enjoyed, he realized that moving up the ladder and getting paid more wouldn't bring him satisfaction. Instead, it was helping others that excited him.

Creating Your Consideration Set

Use your understanding of your own values as a basis for developing the list of jobs you will apply for. The advantage of starting with values is that most of the planning people do is quite specific. They focus on particular jobs and career paths rather than on broader goals based on values. As a result, they take a particular job without ensuring that it will place them on a potentially fulfilling trajectory.

For example, many undergraduate majors are focused on specific career paths. Mechanical engineering feeds into one set of jobs, while computer science directs students toward another set. Often people shy away from majoring in the liberal arts because few jobs obviously lead directly from those concentrations. Some history majors will become academic historians, but most won't—and most companies don't have much call for historians. That doesn't mean a major in history isn't valuable. It teaches many skills—methods of thinking, analyzing situations, and writing—that make students effective at work. But its benefits come from applying those skills rather than from the content of the discipline itself.

Use that capacity for mental time travel that I discussed earlier, and project yourself into the future, looking back on your career. What do you want to say you did? What kinds of things will give you satisfaction?

The trick is not to edit your life story in the forward direction. We all have ideas about how our lives should go. We've imagined where we might live, the jobs we might take, and our ideal family situation. When it comes to a career, too much advance editing of your opportunities will lead you to focus on jobs that fit the ideal you set for yourself. The closer a particular job opportunity is to your vision for your life, the more you may be inclined to apply for and pursue it.

An imagined future, though, is highly constrained by what you already know. Tom Ward and colleagues did studies asking adults to draw creatures from an alien planet. So, the task really called for doing something novel. Nonetheless, participants generally drew things with symmetrical arms and legs and eyes and ears. And the more intelligent the creatures were supposed to be, the more likely they were to walk on two legs. Without realizing it, participants were using their existing knowledge about animals (and which animals are intelligent) as the basis for these new ideas. Any creative pursuit is affected by what you already know.

Your vision for your future works the same way. What you can imagine for yourself is based on things you've experienced already. The career paths you might take are influenced by the career paths you've seen before. That's why my high school self answered the career survey as if I would someday be an accountant. If you edit out potential jobs just because you never envisioned yourself in them, you aren't allowing the world to broaden your base of knowledge about what your career might be. Had I edited my career in advance, you wouldn't be reading this book today. I might be doing your taxes instead.

There are many ways to get exposure to jobs you haven't considered before. Communities often hold career fairs, particularly when colleges or universities are nearby. Many cities have networking groups for people who are job hunting. A career coach can suggest new possibilities. Some websites for job seekers routinely post articles about companies and jobs that fit values such as good work-life balance or career development. Use these resources to expand the options you're willing to consider.

The last big question when compiling your consideration set is how wide a net you want to cast. Should you stick fairly close to the jobs that constitute your ideal, or should you apply to a wider range?

This is one of the few questions about jobs that has a general answer. You should apply for a lot more jobs than you think you need to. Part of the reason you underestimate how many to apply for is that you're editing some out according to beliefs about what you will enjoy. Perhaps more important is that you may be too confident about the likelihood you'll get one of the ones you apply for.

If you're like most other people, you have an *illusion of control*. This term was first used by Ellen Langer, who demonstrated that people believe their actions will have a greater impact on outcomes than they actually do. In the context of jobs you apply for, many factors are completely beyond your control. The company may already have someone in mind for that position. The individual reading your application may not pay careful attention to it. The most recent hire may have gone to the same college you did, and the company had a bad experience with that person.

The process of applying for jobs is a lot more random than you may believe. In most situations, we use the word *randomness* to refer to factors that can't be predicted on the basis of knowledge. As a general rule, then, you should revisit the resources you used to create a list of openings to apply for and include some that you initially eliminated. If you double the length of your original list, you're probably in the right ballpark.

Many job seekers use a different strategy to begin, narrowly focusing on the jobs they think they really want and only gradually broadening the number they consider. There are a few reasons to apply more broadly from the beginning. First, because of factors outside your control, a short list of applications is unlikely to yield a job (or even an interview). That can be demoralizing. Second, an *opportunity cost* is attached to the length of your job search. Opportunity costs are things you could have done with a resource you spent in some other way. If you spend a lot of time waiting for responses to a small number of applications that seemed ideal for you, you'll miss out on other jobs you could have applied for. And the longer you go without working, the more money you could have earned at any job while you were focused on getting the *ideal* job. Third, applying for a job doesn't obligate you to take it. If you get an offer for one that you're not entirely sure you'll like, you can always turn it down. And finally, it's never a bad idea to practice honing your interview skills, even if you end up deciding against the job. In chapter 3, I talk about interviewing for jobs.

For all these reasons, apply for more jobs than you think you need to, and apply for any job you think you could learn to love.

JAZZ BRAIN:
Being Open to New Things

To generate a large consideration set, you have to cultivate *openness*. This is where your jazz brain kicks in. Jazz musicians have to learn to play things that are "outside"—that is, notes in a solo that don't quite fit the chord progression. They do this by playing musical scales (such as the chromatic and diminished scales) that are not central to popular music. Over time, these discordant notes come to feel right, because the scales become familiar. But that happens only because effective improvisers are open to the possibility that melodies can be developed in many ways. Openness doesn't apply just to music. It applies to every potential experience.

Personality psychologists have identified five core characteristics they cleverly call *the Big Five*. One of these is openness to experience, which reflects the orientation people take toward new situations. If you pursue new opportunities with excitement, you are open; if you are anxious about new things, you are closed. Personality is not destiny, though. Even if your natural reaction to new things is to be fearful, you can decide to try them anyhow—particularly when it comes to the workplace.

The reason to cultivate a willingness to explore new things is that many routes to developing a career will match your values. Some may involve jobs you never before considered for yourself. Chris had probably never contemplated life in a war zone before taking that government test, but ultimately he pursued a career he found rewarding.

THE TAKEAWAYS

Your Brains

Motivational Brain

- Feelings are how the motivational system communicates with the brain.
- Emotions are the interpretation of feelings.
- Openness to experience reflects your orientation toward new things.

Social Brain

- Your value system comes in large part from your culture and the people around you. Values may differ significantly between individuals.

Cognitive Brain

- Imagination is driven by what you know.
- You have an illusion of control.

Your Tips

- You don't have to find your passion; you can learn to love your job.
- Seeing your job as a vocation or a calling can help you engage with it.
- Look for jobs that align with your values.
- Don't edit your career in the forward direction.
- Apply for more jobs than you think you need to.
- Don't dismiss job opportunities just because you don't know much about them.

3

Applying and Interviewing

Once you've decided what jobs to apply for, the real fun begins. Now it's time to make contact. This chapter focuses on how to create the best impression at this stage. It starts with the application and extends through the job interview.

Success at this point requires thinking like a recruiter. After all, your application will be evaluated by one or a small number of individuals who will look at your materials, probably without asking you for additional information. The more you know about the way you will be judged, the more likely you are to transition from a few pages in a stack of applications to a personal connection in an interview. The interview has its own dynamic that influences the likelihood you'll get a job offer.

The application process is also a significant chance for you to learn about the company you might work for. Often, applicants treat their applications and interviews as if information flows only from the applicant to the prospective employer. But employers tell you a tremendous amount about their values and what working for them is like through the way they hire. It's important to pay attention to these signals.

Your Application

Most job applications consist of a set of papers (or computer files) that provide your primary opportunity to impress a recruiter or a recruiting committee. They may include an application form, a cover letter that allows you to present your qualifications for the job, a brief résumé highlighting your key experience, and possibly a portfolio of relevant work you've done. Some companies may also ask you to take some tests. These may evaluate skills related to the job or they may be interest and personality inventories.

Your success with this application depends on impressing the recruiters, so you need to know a few things about how people use the materials you provide to make decisions.

Perhaps the most important thing you should determine is what the hiring organization really wants. That means you have a lot of work to do before you even start to put your application materials together.

I spoke to Alison, who has evaluated job applicants and given advice to countless others. She said, "Research, research, research . . . knowing as much as you can about the people, place, culture, to determine if it will be the right fit and what the challenges and oppor-tunities are—not just looking at publicly available and public-facing information, but doing a bit of behind-the-scenes work to get people's impressions from both the inside and the outside. And tailoring your résumé, not just your cover letter, for the job."

The hiring organization provides some amount of information about what it is and what it wants just in the advertisement for a posi-tion. You shouldn't focus only on what the ad says, though. You should also get a good sense of what the organization does and how it talks about its mission. This information is available on its website and can be found in news stories about the company. And if you know people who have worked for the organization (or better yet, still work there), listen to the words they use to talk about their experience.

I spoke to many recruiters in the course of putting together this book, and every single one said that the biggest mistake an applicant can make is to be unfamiliar with the mission of the organization and unclear about what the job ad said. That doesn't mean you'll necessarily know all the tasks the organization has in mind for the position, but it does mean you should be aware of everything that was communicated about it.

You aren't just trying to understand the organization's goals abstractly. The specific language people use is important. One factor that increases people's sense that they like something is the ease with which they can think about it. This ease is called *processing fluency*. Above and beyond what you say about yourself, the more fluently people can process the information you present, the more they will like your application.

How can you ease processing fluency when applying for a job? Repeating the words the organization uses to describe itself and the position is a great start. Robin, who often recruits for startup companies (and has had to apply for a number of jobs over the years), makes this point. He says, "In résumés and interviews I use the same language [the employer] uses. The same thing can be conveyed in so many different ways. If you describe what they want but in your own words, you run a greater risk that they won't realize you're exactly what they're looking for." He suggests that another benefit of using the same language is that recruiters will process your writing more fluently, so they will like it better.

As you put together your materials, you should also pay attention to the latest trends in formatting. Check out online style guides for résumés to find out what fonts people are using, the preferred format, and (if you need to print a hard copy of your materials), the kinds of paper people are using. While you're at it, be sure you don't make any typos.

You might think that the substance of what you have to say is more important than how it looks. But first impressions matter a lot. Much of the information in a résumé and cover letter is not actually that helpful to a recruiter. For entry-level jobs, few applicants are likely to have much relevant experience. For more-advanced jobs, it's hard to compare the experience of various people. Most letters of recommendation are fairly strong, so they don't help to distinguish among the applicants. Sloppy formatting or misspelled words make it easy for a recruiter to give your application only brief consideration.

It's worth saying a bit more about each of these aspects.

Accepting and Rejecting: Beware the Presenter's Paradox

At each stage of the application process, recruiters think differently. Put yourself in their position for a moment. They advertised a job, and lots of people sent in materials. At this preliminary stage, the recruiters' goal is to winnow down the initial applicants to a manageable number that they can look at in more detail.

Even though recruiters ultimately want to find a great candidate, their first task is to reject as many applications as possible. Studies by Eldar Shafir suggest that people tend to give weight to information that is most compatible with the task they are performing at that moment, regardless of their overall goal. That means the first pass at evaluating your application will be looking almost exclusively for information that will enable the recruiter to reject you. Any red flag can keep you out of the pile that gets further review—even if your strengths rival those of the best candidates in the pool.

The first thing you must do is avoid giving any obvious reasons for rejecting your application. Proofread all your materials. It's fairly easy to catch spelling errors, because most word processors highlight them. But read over your application anyhow. You might misuse common words—such as *they're* versus *there* versus *their.* You must make sure that the names of the position, the company, and the contact person in your cover letter are updated for each application. Addressing a cover letter to the head of HR at another company is a great way to land your application in the wastebasket.

The formatting of your materials may matter as well. A résumé that's hard to read can lead a busy recruiter to reject it. Even a poor font choice (Comic Sans, I'm looking at you) can be a problem. Make sure you have eliminated factors that might keep you out of the next round.

You also want to take an honest look at the job description. If some qualifications are listed as necessary, make sure you actually have them. In this first stage of the process, recruiters aren't looking at all the other amazing things you've done. They are using required qualifications to filter the applications.

Luckily, once recruiters finish weeding, their mindset shifts. The compatibility principle I mentioned a few paragraphs ago leads them away from finding reasons to reject applications and toward finding reasons to put people on the short list that will get significant scrutiny and (potentially) an interview. They begin to focus on an application's positive aspects. That means your materials should maximize the impact of the positive information.

Be aware of the *presenter's paradox,* a term coined in a paper by Kimberlee Weaver, Stephen Garcia, and Norbert Schwarz. These researchers point out that when figuring out how to present information about themselves, people tend to throw in every positive thing they can think of. Some of the achievements you highlight may be really great—such as winning an award in college or being recognized by a national panel of experts for an innovation. Others may be good but not great—for instance, honorable mention in a pitch competition.

When you're preparing your materials, you may assume that you'll be evaluated using an *additive* strategy. In other words, the people reading your application will add each accomplishment you present to your total goodness. If your application were being evaluated that way, even an honorable mention would increase the strength of it.

But in fact people making evaluations average together the information they get. So three big achievements plus a few lesser accomplishments may actually result in a lower average than three big achievements alone. Be selective about the positive information you present. Focus on your greatest strengths. Resist the temptation to cram your résumé full of mildly positive elements. Less is more.

Make Your Strengths Clear

Often, people putting together applications assume that others will understand the significance of everything they present. As a result, they miss opportunities to highlight their strengths.

One problem is cultural. Your social brain has probably been programmed to avoid boasting (particularly if you're a woman). It's unseemly to tout your accomplishments in public. You run the risk of alienating other people or getting negative feedback if you spend too much time talking about what a great job you've done. Modesty is the best policy most of the time.

But not when you're applying for a job.

Job applications are not the place to undersell your achievements. If you led a team that succeeded at a venture that several groups had failed at before, make that clear. You're allowed to say things on your application that you would never say about yourself in any other context. Describe your accomplishments in all their glory, and make it abundantly clear what role you played in your team's success.

Again, you have to put yourself in the position of the people reading your application. Recruiters have a large stack of applications to consider, and they may well be trying to fill many positions at the same time. They are looking at a lot of résumés. You cannot assume that a recruiter will understand the significance of your achievements without some guidance. (If you win a Nobel Prize, you probably don't have to spell out why that's noteworthy.)

Suppose a professional society that you belong to has named you as a fellow. Is that a big deal? Perhaps. If the society is the biggest one in your field, and if only a small percentage of the members reach that status, then it's a real mark of distinction, and you ought to annotate this award to let recruiters know that it matters. "Only five percent of the more than 10,000 members of the Really Important Professional Society are named fellows."

You want recruiters to focus on the most important elements of your application as quickly as possible. Highlight key strengths in your cover letter. Relate those strengths to the particular skills that were listed in the job description. Reinforce them in your résumé by using the same words you used in your cover letter to describe them. In this way you will help the recruiter interpret the information in your application.

Your aim is to be called in for an interview. Quite a bit of research in psychology (well summarized in a paper by Eldar Shafir, Itamar Simonson, and Amos Tversky) has focused on *reason-based choice.* In many situations, particularly when people will have to justify the choices they make to others, they seek a reason for those choices—a brief statement of why they chose as they did.

Certainly people make choices in life for which they don't give clear reasons. They might select a piece of artwork for their home because they like it but be unable to say why it attracts them. They might bet on a particular horse because it feels right. But recruiters will most likely have to justify their choice to someone else or on forms documenting the search. Help them construct that reason throughout your packet of materials.

Finally, be aware that you must be able to back up any claims you make in your application. The number of high-profile cases in which prominent people have falsified credentials makes it worth reiterating that any concrete elements on your résumé should be as accurate as possible. If you attended a particular school without graduating from it, don't list yourself as a graduate. If you received honorable mention for a prize, don't list yourself as a winner.

More important, perhaps, be realistic about your accomplishments. Research on *egocentric bias* suggests that people generally overestimate the importance of their own contributions to the success of a venture. Indeed, if you asked everyone on a team to assess the percentage of effort they contributed toward a final product, the total would be far more than 100 percent.

Nothing is inherently wrong with overestimating the importance of your contribution in the context of a job application, but be sure that you can provide specific examples of what you did. If you are selected to interview for a position you applied for, the recruiter is quite likely to ask you to talk in more detail about the accomplishments you highlighted in your application. You must have specific evidence or anecdotes to illustrate your claims.

The Interview

After you send off your materials comes a frustrating waiting game in which everything is outside your control. The recruiters are evaluating a stack of applications to determine whom they want to meet personally. That is where the interview process begins.

Interviews are labor-intensive for recruiters, so usually they bring in only a few people for each position they have to fill. When you get an interview, you should feel good. Your chances of getting a job offer have just gone up substantially.

Interviews have a big influence on whether you get a job offer, even though it's unclear just how much valuable information they provide to a prospective employer. An applicant's résumé spans an entire career.

It includes statements of qualifications, certifications, and education history. References reflect reasonably long-term relationships. If the application includes a portfolio, the work provided reflects substantial effort. But an interview is often only a few hours long (or at most a few days, for very high-level positions) and conducted in a highly controlled environment. It's not obvious that this small sample of information about a candidate ought to outweigh the information on an application.

Perhaps business can learn a bit from the restaurant industry. My middle son works in restaurant kitchens. When he applies for a new job, he has a brief interview, his references are checked, and then he works all or part of a shift (called a *stage*, from the French word *stagiaire*, or "trainee"). This trial by fire provides information to both employers and candidates. Employers get a look at candidates' skills, and candidates get a sense of whether the kitchen is one they would mesh with and enjoy. More than once, my son has done a stage at a restaurant only to decide that it isn't a place he wants to work, even though it's willing to give him the job.

What do employers hope to get from an interview? For one thing, they want information about your skills that may not have been clear from your application. A growing number of firms also use the interview as an opportunity to give tests that may indicate your aptitude for certain positions. In addition, they are trying to assess your fit with the organization. Are you likely to be good to work with? One recruiter I spoke to said that a big part of the interview was making sure the candidate didn't have four heads and spit fire.

But you can learn a lot about your prospective employer through the interview process, just as my son learned a lot about each restaurant from doing a stage. Many people are so concerned with making a good impression at the interview that they don't think about what they might learn.

Let's look at some aspects of the interview in more detail.

Skills

It can be hard to get a true sense of your skills from a résumé. You may have some certifications that attest to particular technical abilities, but even then it's not always obvious what you're capable of doing. So companies may devote part of the interview time to assessing your skills.

In technical fields, they may ask you to solve specific problems within the areas of expertise that the job requires. Joy was applying for a data analysis job at a big firm, and they sent her several sample problems to solve after an initial screening interview. She then discussed her responses with the interviewer at a second visit. Companies may also ask you to make recommendations on the basis of your knowledge or to predict how much time a particular project would take.

Similar questions may be asked in other fields. Teachers may be asked to develop a lesson plan or to explain how they would deal with a particular classroom situation. Salespeople may be asked to talk through an approach to a hypothetical client. Many of the popular employment websites have sections where people who have interviewed with companies post questions they were asked. Look through these questions to get a sense of what might come up during the interview. If you know anyone with experience at the company, you might run some of your potential answers past them for feedback.

Interviewers are trying to learn about you by asking these questions. Part of what they want to know, of course, is whether you have represented your skills accurately on your résumé. They are also trying to get a sense of how you approach problems. Here are a few things to consider.

First, don't panic if you aren't immediately sure how to answer a question. Interviews are stressful situations, and research on the cognitive brain suggests that stress decreases the amount of information you can hold in your mind—what is called your *working memory capacity*.

Working memory is important for solving complex problems, so stress can make it harder for you to succeed at the problems you're given. If you panic, you'll feel even more stress, and your working memory capacity will decrease further.

Second, remember that many companies develop their own terminology for talking about things relating to their business. Suppose you were interviewing for a position at Procter & Gamble, and you were asked about strategies for improving performance of a product at the first moment of truth. You might be unsure how to approach this question, because "the first moment of truth"—the company's in-house term for the first few seconds of the interaction between a customer and a product on the store shelf—is a phrase not commonly used outside P&G.

If an interviewer uses a term unfamiliar to you, it's OK to ask for clarification. Don't assume that every jargon term an interviewer employs is in common use. It's important to make sure you understand the question you are being asked.

Third, you should feel free to use questions as an opportunity to engage in a conversation with the interviewer. For example, if you're asked to estimate how much time a project might take, ask what tools the company routinely uses for project scheduling and what groups usually meet to go over deadlines and responsibilities. Such questions show that you're familiar with the key barriers to solving the problem you've been asked about and want to learn how the company addresses them.

At one time, companies also asked very general kinds of reasoning and logic questions at interviews. Google, for example, was famous for asking interviewees to solve outlandish puzzles. This technique has fallen out of favor, however, because the ability to solve problems with no connection to real situations does not predict how well an applicant will perform in a job. Real problem solving is a knowledge-intensive process.

Traits

A number of companies also test for traits to match people with jobs. A *trait* is a long-term motivation that affects your behavior—as opposed to a *state*, which is a motivation or a feeling you experience in the moment in a given situation. As part of an application or interview process, you may be asked to respond to several questionnaires that aim to assess core personality characteristics.

Throughout this book, I talk about a variety of traits that relate to performance in the workplace. For now, though, I want to make three key points.

First, your personality characteristics reflect the default settings of your motivational brain. Each person's motivational system is wired slightly differently, with different preferences. Some people gravitate toward social interactions, while others prefer to work individually. Some are motivated to think things over carefully, while others prefer to do something and see what happens.

Once you reach adulthood, these default motivations remain fairly stable over the course of your life. If you generally prefer to work alone, you are unlikely to suddenly become motivated to engage in lots of social interactions at work. That's why it can be useful for companies to do these assessments. They provide a snapshot of some general factors that affect your motivational brain.

It's in your best interests to answer the questions on personality inventories as accurately as you can. Companies that use them well are trying to ensure that you don't end up in a role that you'll find grating because it asks you to consistently fly in the face of your default motivation. It isn't worth trying to guess what kind of responses a company wants on these questionnaires, because you might be offered a position that isn't well suited to your traits.

Second, personality traits are not destiny. Most studies of personality suggest that people's differences in a particular trait predict at most about 20 percent of their differences in a specific behavior, because many factors determine what you do. A situation itself often guides your behavior. Your goals affect you as well. As a result, you may perform a number of tasks at work that are incompatible with your personality traits and still love those tasks because you believe in your organization's mission, are excited about the goal you're achieving, or care about your coworkers.

That means you should pay attention to the results you get on personality tests but not use them as the sole reason for decisions about your career. Your traits are just one of many factors that affect your success in a position.

Finally, be wary of any organization that gives you the Myers-Briggs Type Indicator (MBTI) as part of the interview process. A popular inventory, the MBTI classifies people along four dimensions that are rooted in the psychological theories of Karl Jung. Unfortunately, the MBTI has a number of problems. In particular, its test-retest reliability is low, meaning that if you take it several times, you may get very different results. Because it fails to predict behavior consistently, it rarely appears in scientific studies of behavior. And the MBTI makes you appear more extreme on the four dimensions than you really are, because a lot of personality research suggests that most people fall toward the middle of them. If an organization gives you this test as part of its hiring process, it doesn't have people on staff who truly understand how personality traits should be used in the workplace.

Social Skills

One thing it's impossible to tell from a résumé is what a person is really like to be around. That information is valuable, because central to the success of any workplace is the degree to which people get along and work together to accomplish key tasks. If your job will require a lot of group problem solving, and the specific tasks of it are constantly evolving according to what your teammates are doing, the company needs to know that you can play well with others.

Even candidates who on paper have all the skills needed for the job may be a bad fit if they're unlikely to get along with their coworkers or to resonate with the corporate culture. For this reason, recruiters assess your social abilities. Lucas told a story that summarizes this. When he went to his second interview at a company, he was told that the first interview had been designed to determine his ability to do the job, and the second was meant to "make sure [he] wasn't an asshole."

For this aspect of the interview, you want to display an authentic business self. That may seem obvious, but interviews are stressful situations; you may not think carefully about how you want to come across. You may end up saying or doing something that you later regret. So here are a few things to bear in mind.

Your appearance at the interview really does matter. A lot of work has been done on *thin-slice judgments* demonstrating that people make up their minds quickly about a person they meet. Some of their impression comes from engaging with the person, but some comes from their appearance. Does the person look like someone they would be comfortable with?

Anything about your appearance that calls attention to itself may negatively influence people's initial impression of you. And that impression can affect how people evaluate the things you do during an interview. Just as there is potential ambiguity in the factors you list on your résumé, there is ambiguity in understanding your behavior. Was a comment you made funny or snarky? Confident or arrogant? Charming or sucking up? Someone with a favorable initial impression of you is likely to interpret your behavior charitably. When people have a positive impression of you, they tend to interpret your behavior more positively, which leads to more favorable judgments about you. This phenomenon is called the *halo effect*.

When advising people about interviews, several of them have argued that they should be able to display their authentic selves at all times—even during an interview. I hate to sound like a dinosaur, but dressing professionally is not inauthentic, even if it's not how you normally dress. It simply demonstrates that you understand enough about the context of an interview to let it guide your behavior. There will be many times during your work life when you won't say what's really on your mind or do a particular project exactly the way you wanted to do it. Dressing well during your interview shows that you understand the rules governing work behavior—even if you never again have to dress well for work again.

The people you meet are likely to remember only a small amount of information about their encounter with you later—usually about three things. If one of them is an aspect of your appearance, the other two had better be really good.

You should also do what you can to enhance the impression your interviewer gets. Martin Pickering and Simon Garrod have reviewed a lot of evidence that people mirror one another during social interactions. If you smile, your conversation partners are likely to smile. If you lean forward, they will lean forward. If you engage with energy, they will as well. If you project enthusiasm, joy, and energy, it will rub off onto your interviewer.

Being energetic is even more crucial in an interview than in a typical social interaction, because it's quite likely that the person who interviews you is engaging in a whole day (perhaps even many days) of interactions with potential candidates. It can be hard for interviewers to stay engaged for every interview. If you're the last one before lunch, you may find that your interviewer's enthusiasm is flagging—which can lead you to display low energy as well. So bring your own energy and carry the interviewer along.

Speaking of lunch, prepare yourself for any meals you may have during a recruiting visit. If you have dietary restrictions, let the people coordinating your interview know about them ahead of time. Eat slowly. If you eat less at an interview than you normally would, that's fine. And be judicious about alcohol. If you normally have a drink with dinner, take the lead from your hosts. But stop at one drink no matter what they are doing.

Be personable, but stick to the kinds of interactions that you're most comfortable with. If you don't generally try to be funny, don't test out a comic persona for the first time in an interview. Don't trot out new entries in your vocabulary—you may use words incorrectly or pronounce them wrong. Impress people by being the best version of yourself, not the person you think the company wants you to be.

That said, try to sand off any rough edges in your interactions with people. If you tend to be blunt or opinionated about your industry or current events, you may want to leave such opinions aside until after you're hired.

Most important, focus on the positive. It's easy to get into a spiral of criticizing others and making disparaging comments. It can feel empowering to criticize, but you may say something negative about something the interviewer feels strongly about. Success in the workplace involves not just identifying problems but generating solutions. Getting stuck in a cycle of criticism may obscure your ability to solve problems. Finally, the more negative a conversation you have with someone, the more concepts and feelings are negative in their mind as they talk to you. Some of that negativity may attach to you, ultimately decreasing how much you are liked.

Your goal is to be the kind of person the company wants to spend more time with. You may object that you should display your true self—warts and all. Your friends love your bluntness, your offbeat sense of humor, or your tendency to create awkward silences. And your colleagues may come to enjoy them as well after they get to know you. But you don't need to highlight your interpersonal foibles on the first day.

JAZZ BRAIN:

After You Blow a Note, It Is Gone

When I first started learning to play jazz on the saxophone, I blew a lot of sour notes. A lot. Usually I would stop after messing up, particularly during lessons when I was trying to show off. In those moments, my teacher would put his hand to his ear and say, "Hear that? No! That note is gone. Now play."

You're going to make mistakes in job interviews. You're going to answer a question less well than you could have. You're going to blank on something you should have known.

No company is looking for perfection. What it does want is to know how you're going to face adversity. Don't let the rest of the interview suffer from an earlier mistake. Research on performance under pressure (much of it reviewed in Sian Beilock's wonderful book *Choke*) suggests that you start paying a lot of attention to your own actions when the stakes are high. But you can't have a natural conversation when you're focused too closely on every aspect of what you're doing.

By the time you get to an interview, you have to trust in your preparation. If you make a mistake, just let it go and continue to interact normally with your interviewer. You can think about how to improve the way you answer questions later, when the interview is over.

What Should You Be Learning?

It's easy to walk into an interview fixated on how you're going to be judged. After all, you have a lifetime of practice at being evaluated by other people. You know that when you take an exam, it's all about your performance.

But interviews are bidirectional. If you've gotten to the point where you're being interviewed, the company has some interest in you.

Although you're trying to impress the interviewer, this is also their opportunity to show you what it's like to work for this company. Don't miss out on that.

For example, Lisa told me, "Whenever I go to an interview and there is a surprise task, I turn down the job. Those people will not respect you or your time." Regardless of how you yourself feel about such surprises, the key point here is that the company is showing something about the way it treats employees through the way it handles an interview.

Some of what you learn from the interview should come explicitly through the questions you ask. Consult as many resources as possible about the firm you're interviewing with. Find out what positive and negative things people say about working there before you get to the interview. Come prepared with questions about what it's like to be an employee. Such preparation is valuable because it demonstrates that you're seriously interested in the job.

Certainly, specific answers to your questions matter; but how they're answered matters as well. If you raise a criticism other people have made about working for the company, find out how willingly it will admit to past complaints. True *learning organizations* embrace criticisms made in the past and talk about how they've attempted to improve the work environment. Companies that brush off criticism are often unwilling to change even after you arrive.

A lot of what you can learn about a firm, though, comes from observing the interview itself. Consider a situation in which the interviewer stumps you with a question. Perhaps you're asked how you would approach a particular interaction with a client. You aren't sure, so you ask some questions to clarify and possibly even ask how the interviewer would handle it. You might think that you've blown the answer, spelling doom for your chances of being hired.

Some companies assume that you come equipped with all the skills you need to do your job. Others invest in your potential. They see you as someone who can work with others and solve problems. If you haven't yet mastered some bit of knowledge or a particular skill, they treat that as an opportunity to develop you further. An interviewer who frowns and downgrades you for not knowing an answer is communicating that the firm wants a fully formed employee from day one. An interviewer who is willing to engage in a discussion about a hard problem and teach during the interview is communicating that the firm believes in growing the capacities of its employees. One of my early interview experiences was for a sales associate position at a retail electronics chain when I was in college. The interviewer was the district manager. When it became clear I didn't know much about sales, he spent the interview teaching me about how to interact with customers. And I got the job.

From this perspective, it can actually be valuable to have a (mildly) negative interaction at some point during the interview. Not every day at work is going to be bliss. At times a project will go badly or you'll make a mistake. Organizations that allow you to recover from a mistake during the interview are showing you what they believe brings success. For many people, an organization that supports their growth provides a satisfying work environment. Look for information during the interview about how organizations handle these situations. If you have no negative interactions during the interview, that's great—but then ask questions about training opportunities for employees. Talk specifically about what happens when someone makes a mistake. Find out whether the HR process allows for a development plan to improve your skills.

To maximize what you learn about the organization from the interview, get your cognitive brain ready. Make a list of the biggest unknowns about the organization, and bring it to the interview. Read it over before the interview starts so that you're primed to pick up on information related to those unknowns. Make notes during the interview as well—don't rely on your memory. Keep track of things an interviewer says that strike you as particularly important.

This list can be particularly helpful if you get an offer, because you'll have to negotiate the terms of your position before deciding whether to take the job. Chapter 4 explores that part of the process, but it's important to remember that the recruitment process has actually started with the interview.

After the Interview

When the interview is over, don't forget to send an email thanking the recruiters for their time. If you're excited about the position, say that as well. Your email will keep the lines of communication open in case the recruiters have any issues they want to follow up about.

After that, though, you have to be patient. Feel free to ask during the interview when a decision is likely so that you'll have some idea of what to expect. Bear in mind that the process of filling one or more jobs at an organization is time-consuming. It's not up to the company to relieve your anxiety about the job search.

The only time you should reach out again to a recruiter while you're waiting is when some significant new information comes up. Suppose, for example, you applied for a patent at your previous job and the patent has come through. This information may be valuable to the new firm, so you might send it a note with an updated résumé. Similarly, if you're particularly interested in one job and you receive another offer, you can let the company know that you're entertaining another offer and hope to hear from it before your deadline.

It's hard to just sit and wait, though; the decision process is utterly out of your control after you complete your interview, and that's frustrating and anxiety-provoking. Your motivational brain wants to have a certain amount of *agency*. It's natural to wish to somehow reassert control. In this case, though, you're better off letting the process play out. If you approach recruiters at this stage, you're likely to just annoy them, which cannot help your application.

THE TAKEAWAYS

Your Brains

Motivational Brain

- Stress decreases *working memory capacity*.

Social Brain

- Beware of the *presenter's paradox*. People average, they don't add.
- Watch out for *egocentric bias*. You probably overestimate your own contribution to projects.
- The *halo effect* occurs when people judge someone's deeds charitably because they received a good initial impression of them.
- People mirror one another in social interactions.

Cognitive Brain

- *Processing fluency* is the ease with which people comprehend information.
- There are *task compatibility* effects in choice: When rejecting applications, people focus on the negative. When accepting applications, they focus on the positive.
- People want reasons for many of the choices they make.

Your Tips

- Do a lot of research on the firms you apply to.
- Use the same language recruiters use to improve processing fluency.
- Proofread carefully. Avoid obvious reasons for rejecting your application.

- Focus on putting your best foot forward. Don't highlight mediocre aspects of your record.

- Don't undersell your achievements, but do be specific about what you've done.

- If you get nervous during an interview, remember to ask questions.

- Be prepared to demonstrate the skills you highlight in your application.

- Present your authentic business self at the interview.

- Bring energy and enthusiasm to the interview, and your interviewer will mirror that.

- Don't worry about mistakes you make at the interview. You may learn something about how the organization deals with error.

- Come prepared with questions for the interviewer.

- After the interview, be patient.

4

From the Offer
to the Decision

After you finish the interview process, you'll eventually hear back from the organizations you met. Logically speaking, of course, there are only two possibilities: an offer or news that you didn't get the job. This chapter focuses on the time between when you hear back from an organization and when you decide whether to accept an offer.

I'll start by talking briefly about what to do when you don't get a job you wanted. Most of this chapter, though, will focus on how to negotiate with an organization most effectively and ways to think about your decision.

First, the Bad News

Your motivational brain engages with goals that are important to you. For many people involved in a job search, few goals are more important than getting a particular job. They are deeply invested in that goal.

Your degree of engagement with a goal determines the strength of your emotional reaction relating to it. Whether that reaction is positive or negative depends on whether you succeed or fail. I used to be a huge sports fan, so when the New York Giants lost a football game, it could ruin my day. But as I have gotten older, my commitment to sports in general has declined. Hearing that the Giants lost a game has at most a mild influence on my emotional state these days.

When you learn that you didn't get a job you really wanted, you'll have a strong negative reaction. You might be sad, anxious, or angry. The particular emotional experience you have depends on how you appraise the situation. As I mentioned in chapter 2, emotion is an interpretation of your feelings. You'll be sad if you focus primarily on the opportunity you lost. You'll be anxious if you focus on your need to get a job. You'll be angry if you think that someone (perhaps the recruiter) did something unfair in the process of making the decision.

For example, I had a discussion with two colleagues who applied for positions at our university. Both were passed over in favor of other candidates, and (predictably) both experienced a significant negative response. One colleague focused on the lost opportunity and so was sad and disappointed for a while after getting the news. The other felt that the hiring committee had failed to recognize a sustained commitment to the university. This colleague experienced a lot of anger toward the committee and the university. The same situation can lead to very different emotional responses depending on your interpretation of what happened.

When you first learn that you didn't get a job, your initial reaction may be to do something about it.

Don't.

When you're feeling strongly negative about some outcome, many actions may seem reasonable in the moment. You may want to fire off an email or make a phone call. You may want to complain loudly to lots of people that you should have gotten the job.

Such reactions are unlikely to help you get a job (at that organization or anywhere else) in the long term. And when it comes to a career, you have to be willing to play the long game.

So the first thing you need to do is give yourself a chance to calm down. Get some exercise or go dancing to release any energy you have. Do yoga or meditate. Get a good night's sleep before you do anything at all.

A big reason not to complain much is that you never know whether things you say may get back to the organization, and you don't want to burn any bridges. I interviewed at the University of Texas in 1993, and though my interview went quite well, the job was offered to someone else. I kept up my contacts with the department, and five years later, when another position opened up, I was invited to apply. I have now worked there for more than twenty years.

After you've given yourself time to calm down, you can think about whether to reach out to the company that rejected you. If you were part of a large recruitment pool, it may not be helpful to do so, because the recruiters are unlikely to remember you well. But if you feel that you made a personal connection with the recruiters (and the job was one you were really interested in), it might be worthwhile to reiterate your interest in the organization and ask for some feedback about how you could improve in future interviews.

By asking for ways to improve, you're not implying that the recruiter made a mistake—you're demonstrating that you're interested in learning how to get better at the things you do. Sometimes you can get useful feedback from these interactions. At worst, you will have reminded the recruiter that you're quite interested. Indeed, my oldest son (mentioned in chapter 1) was at first rejected by the company he eventually went to work for. He reached out for feedback because he thought the interview had gone pretty well. During that call, the recruiter decided to bring him in for a second interview and then hired him.

The main thing to remember is that every interaction you have with an organization affects your social network. You want to increase the number of people who have a positive opinion of you and minimize the number of people who don't. This is particularly important to bear in mind when you're experiencing strong negative emotions.

Negotiation Time

And then there's the day you get a call saying that you're being offered a job. You'll still feel a strong reaction, but it's likely to be one of happiness, joy, and excitement—perhaps tempered with nervousness.

You have some work to do before you're ready to actually sign on the dotted line. You have to negotiate the terms of your employment. You have more leverage at this point than you're likely to have for some time to come. The firm has said that it wants you to work there, and now it's in recruiting mode. Once you accept the job, you won't have the same power to negotiate until it's clear that you might move elsewhere or your performance has gotten so good that your employer wants to reward you. So this is the time to create a situation that will help you achieve your goals.

The first thing you need to do is engage your cognitive brain and prepare for the negotiation.

Fixing the Information Asymmetry

The fundamental difficulty with negotiating is the information asymmetry between you and the firm that wants to hire you. You know your own needs and what you would accept for salary, benefits, start date, signing bonus, and vacation. The company knows who it has as backup in case the negotiation with you falls through, how much it normally pays for positions like the one you're being offered, and the range of other ways it compensates employees, such as year-end bonuses, commission rates for salespeople, and education benefits. Unless your offer is from a very small firm, it also has a lot more experience negotiating terms of employment than you do. That means your first task is to reduce the information asymmetry by learning as much as you can about the company you're negotiating with.

To overcome this asymmetry, take a systematic approach to preparing for your negotiation. Do not rely on your intuition about when you're ready. Lots of research on *construal level* suggests that things that are distant in time, space, or social relationships are conceptualized more abstractly than things that are up close.

When you're distant from actually working at a company, you are likely to focus on the seemingly most important elements of the job offer, such as salary and vacation time. However, many specific details about a position that may not seem crucial from this distance will become important once you're an employee. These range from the space in which you'll be working (office, cubicle, shared desk) to compensation (retirement plan, bonus structure) to career development (mentoring, education benefits) to hours (flextime, weekend work, overtime), to relocation expenses if you have to move to take the job.

Start by listing all the questions about an employment package that you'll want to consider. After you make your own list of questions, show it to a few other people to make sure you haven't missed anything significant.

After that, you need to answer those questions. You may know how to address a few of these questions from your own experience, but make sure to check other sources as well. Look for connections in the industry (or better still, inside the firm where you have an offer), and learn how similar companies structure their compensation packages. People may not want to tell you their exact salary, but you can discover how their compensation and benefits are set up. Many companies want to highlight what they offer, so you can also ask the recruiter. As I'll discuss in a little while, just because you're negotiating with people doesn't mean they're adversaries.

Next determine what you want to get out of the negotiation. Start by assessing your needs. How much money do you (and others who may depend on your income) need to survive (and thrive) where you'll be living for this job? What aspirations do you have that might change that amount over the next few years? If you and a partner have discussed having children, for example, you should factor that in. Will you be able to save anything for emergencies and future goals?

Think about your ideal work schedule. You may feel most comfortable with the traditional nine-to-five. However, other passions may influence your ideal. Because I play in a band, I know a number of musicians. Many of them have taken jobs that accommodate the late nights common to playing live music. One, for example, is a baker, so he works a shift starting at 3:00 a.m.—just about the time he gets out of a late gig. Others have arranged to start their day jobs at 10:00 a.m. so that they can get a little sleep after a club date.

You also want to prioritize the various aspects of the offer. Which factors are you unwilling to budge on? Which are you willing to trade off? Determine your areas of flexibility in preparing for the negotiation. Perhaps you're willing to trade a little of your salary for a signing bonus that would cover the expense of relocating to a new town. Don't wait until the actual negotiation to contemplate the kinds of trade-offs you're willing to make. Once the negotiation starts, you will feel pressure to make a deal, and you might make concessions you'll regret later.

Now it's time to get specific information related to your needs. What is the salary range for positions like the one you're being offered? Many employment websites will show you typical compensation packages for similar positions, and many of them also break those ranges down by region to take into account cost-of-living factors.

If you know people in the industry, they can provide valuable information—particularly if your online research doesn't turn up any position clearly comparable to the one you're taking. I was talking with D (the name he actually goes by), who retired from the military after a distinguished thirty-year career and went to look for a job in the private sector. He got an offer from a large consulting firm to manage a project it was doing for a military base. It turned out that D knew the primary contact for the military base, so he was able to get information about the size and scope of the contract that supported his salary request, which was ultimately granted.

The goal of all this effort is to minimize the extent to which you're negotiating without any knowledge of the firm's position. You want to know which aspects of the offer are negotiable and to lay out your core needs.

What Is Negotiation?

Before you can negotiate effectively, you have to understand what a negotiation is and how to think about the ideal outcome.

A negotiation is a way of resolving a perceived *conflict of interest*, which is any situation in which the goals of two parties differ. An employee may want to be paid as much as possible for work, while an employer may want to minimize costs. I say "perceived" in this definition because in many situations, one party makes unwarranted assumptions about what the other party wants. A firm may want to keep its employees happy and so may be willing to pay significantly more than the minimum to hire and retain talent.

Most people walk into negotiations with an implicit metaphorical framing for negotiation. Metaphors are ways of talking about the world that conceptualize one domain in terms of another. For example, you might say, "Sarita attacked Juan's arguments until he retreated." If so, you are talking about an argument as if it were a war.

Placing a particular metaphorical frame around a situation often affects how you judge success and failure. Thinking about an argument as a war assumes that if you don't persuade the other side to come to your position, you've lost. Within this frame, reaching a mutual understanding of a complex issue would not be viewed as a positive outcome.

The dominant metaphorical frame for negotiation has two sides sitting across the table from each other with the agreement somewhere on the table between them. If the agreement moves closer to one party, it necessarily moves farther from the other. As a result, the two sides are engaged in a tug-of-war, with each side trying to get the most concessions from the other. In this view, negotiation is fundamentally competitive, so if one side is winning, the other is losing.

A consequence is that each party worries that the other will try to take advantage of any information it gets. So parties often withhold information about what they want or need, assuming that an information asymmetry creates power for their negotiating position.

It's worth considering an alternative metaphorical frame for negotiations in employment contexts. Think about walking side by side with your negotiation partner into a landscape. The negotiated agreement is somewhere out there, and the only constraint is that you must reach it together.

In this view, negotiation is more about joint problem solving than about winning. This approach opens up potential win-win situations in which both parties have the same goal. For example, you might want to take two months off to travel before starting a new job. Your prospective employer might be building out new office space and want a few months before you start. If you assume that the goals of the other side oppose yours, you may not ask for exactly what you want, fearing that the other party will walk away from the table. You might reach a deal that is actually worse for both of you.

In addition, when you treat a negotiation as an opportunity to walk together, you'll disclose information about your needs and wants. Your negotiation partner can't help you reach your goals without knowing what they are. It may be that your partner can't give you what you want the way you want it, but may be able to do so in a different way.

For example, Suzanne was negotiating for a sales job. She was hoping to make a six-figure salary. The company had very little cash available to offer as a base salary, but it was willing to increase the commission to the point where a good performance would allow Suzanne to reach her goal. Working together enabled them to reach an agreement that they would not have gotten to had they not both been clear about their goals and constraints.

The key point here is that an information asymmetry about your real goals does not help in negotiation with a prospective employer. If you want or need something, let the employer know. If what you want or need is inconsistent with the goals and values of the firm and it tells you so, you've learned something valuable. Often, though, your prospective employer has options you're unaware of for reaching your goals in ways you never considered. But you won't find that out unless you tell the employer what you really want.

Launching the Negotiation

How can you get the negotiation started?

One of the most prominent discoveries in psychology over the past fifty years is the *anchoring and adjustment* heuristic first outlined by Amos Tversky and Daniel Kahneman. The idea is quite simple. When trying to place a value on something, people fixate on a number in their mental environment. They may know that the number is wrong and thus adjust it in the direction they think is correct. However, they often adjust insufficiently, misvaluing the item as a result.

As a quick example outside the domain of value, suppose someone asks you what year George Washington was elected president of the United States. The year the Declaration of Independence was signed, 1776, is a prominent historical anchor. You know Washington had to have been elected later than that, so you adjust. However, you're likely to adjust insufficiently, in part because the Revolutionary War was much longer than most more-recent conflicts. You might think that it took about six years, and so guess that Washington was elected in 1783. In fact the Constitutional Convention wasn't held until 1787, and Washington was elected president in 1789.

In negotiations, the first numbers you see or hear can anchor discussion about key values for the rest of the negotiation. Throughout the course of a negotiation, figure out what numbers you may be using as anchors and be careful not to get too attached to them. Connor—a longtime recruiter—talks about a mistake that applicants fresh out of college commonly make. They look at the salary range given by the firm when advertising a position, anchor on the top end of that range, and get angry when the firm tries to negotiate them lower. They may walk away from an offer thinking that the firm is trying to lowball them.

It's important to understand the function of a salary range. The top end tells experienced employees whether this job is a potential move up from their current job—something that can be hard to tell from the job description alone. A top end of $48,000 tells someone already making $52,000 that the job probably isn't a good fit.

The bottom end of the range shows what the company expects to pay someone with little or no experience, such as a recent college graduate. Fixating on the top end of the range when you have no experience is likely to cause you dissatisfaction. Anchor on the bottom end instead and adjust upward to reach the salary you'll ask for.

Another source of anchors in negotiation can come from having a job offer in hand. In negotiation parlance, the other offer is a

BATNA, which stands for "best alternative to a negotiated agreement." If your negotiation with this firm falls through, what's your alternative? If you have another offer in hand, your alternative is to take it. If you don't, your best alternative is to return to your job search.

Obviously, it's more comfortable to be negotiating with a firm if you already have another job offer, because you may feel that you can take some risk in your negotiations over this one. It's also natural to use the offer you have as an anchor—in other words, adjust the salary you've been offered upward as a request to the new firm.

If you adopt this strategy, though, you may inadvertently leave money on the table. The company may actually be willing to pay you much more than you ask for. So make sure you know the salary range for that position. You don't want to anchor on your BATNA when you could have done much better.

Finally, pay attention to how you frame your anchor—and to how numbers are framed when you see them. Suppose you ask for a salary of $51,000. This anchor communicates that you expect the negotiation to focus on the smallest non-zero digit. You expect a counteroffer of $48,000. Notice, though, that you're now talking about some fairly significant money, because $3,000 works out to $250 a month. That's a couple of trips to the grocery store and a night out.

Suppose instead that you ask for $51,400. Now you're communicating that you expect the negotiation to be over hundreds rather than thousands of dollars. Research by Adam Galinsky and colleagues provides some evidence that negotiators are sensitive to these more specific anchors—provided you don't go crazy with them. (Asking for a salary of $51,432.04 won't get you a specific response.) Try an anchor that is one level down from what your intuition tells you to ask for. It may constrain the range of counteroffers you get, landing you right where you wanted to be.

Listen and Learn

A theme of this book is that your social brain can help you learn a lot about your prospective employer. That certainly holds true in the negotiation process. A willingness to negotiate and to look for solutions to any impasses tells you a lot about how flexible the company is willing to be in working with you and how likely it is to seek innovative solutions to problems after you start your job.

Heather told me about an experience she had as a recruiter hired by a high-tech firm to find an executive assistant for the CEO. She found the perfect candidate, who asked for a salary of $65,000. Citing cost-of-living differences between cities, the firm counteroffered $55,000. The candidate did not want to take a pay cut from her previous job and held firm at $65,000. The firm came up to $57,500 with a promise of a $7,500 bonus, but it wouldn't be specific about the criteria required to get the bonus. The candidate was concerned that this reflected a lack of respect for her talent and expertise. She elected to take the job but left soon after, because her experience at the company mirrored what happened during the interview.

Some of the information you get about a company will be positive, of course—even if it doesn't give you everything you asked for. Connor, whom I mentioned in an earlier story, pointed out that many candidates who ask for salaries at the high end of the range even though they have no relevant experience in the industry don't understand how much they'll need to learn to do the job properly. His firm talks to recruits about the amount of training it does during employees' first several years to help them excel at their jobs.

Candidates value this education if they recognize that the firm is investing in their future—if they learn, they will ultimately be able to command a higher salary at this firm or another one. Candidates who fixate on salary alone walk away from Connor's firm. Many of them are hired by companies that don't offer such a generous package of training.

When you first start negotiating with an organization, it's useful to have a mentor who can advise you about how to interpret the situation. Are you being given a good reason why your salary is lower than you would like? Why can't the company be flexible about paid time off? When you don't get what you want in a negotiation, you may blame the firm and assume that something about it makes it uncooperative. It's important to know whether you're missing something crucial that might clarify why your demands weren't reasonable. A more experienced colleague may be able to help you read the tea leaves after a negotiation that didn't go exactly as you'd hoped.

Thinking and Doing at the Right Times

A line of research begun by Arie Kruglanski and Tory Higgins is rooted in the observation that the motivational brain has a *thinking* mode and a *doing* mode. In the thinking mode, you process information about a situation. You are considering options and working through problems. In the doing mode, you prepare for action. You get impatient when you're held back from making progress on something. Metaphors capture this distinction: you may talk about *taking a step back* for more contemplation versus *moving forward* with a plan.

During a negotiation, you need to pay attention to these modes. While you're still trying to improve the deal you're working on, you want to remain in the thinking mode. You're looking for ways to get more of your needs met. When you feel that you've gotten the best deal you can, you want to flip into the doing mode to reach an agreement and sign on the dotted line.

Ideally, that's the way it would work.

But recruiters can manipulate situations to influence your motivational mode. Putting a deadline on an offer is a way to spur action.

The closer you get to the deadline, the more pressure you feel to act rather than think.

You can also negotiate about the deadline, though. Employers feel time pressure. Several candidates may be waiting to hear about a job, and some of them may be people the company would want if you don't take the job. At the same time, employers want you to be fully committed to the job you take so that they won't lose you several months later when a better opportunity comes along.

You should ask for a deadline extension if you need it. When I was a fairly new PhD looking for an academic job, I got an offer from the University of Illinois at Chicago. About a week before I was supposed to make a final decision about that offer, I got a call from Columbia University inviting me to interview for a position there. I contacted the folks at Illinois and asked for an extension. They granted it, because they didn't want me to accept their position under duress. Ultimately, I got the job at Columbia, and Illinois hired someone else.

In addition to circumstances, your own thoughts can influence your motivational mode. Job searches are stressful because they involve a lot of uncertainty. You may just want to get it over with. If you jump into the doing mode, you might start applying for all kinds of jobs and be tempted to take the first offer you get, rather than staying in the thinking mode and waiting before responding to an offer that isn't ideal for you.

This is another time when having someone to advise you can be helpful. When the job market is good, you don't need to leap at the first offer that comes along. It can be hard to stay motivated in a job that is a poor fit for you. And a job whose salary and benefits don't meet your needs is one that you may have to leave sooner rather than later. A good mentor can help you decide when you might be better off waiting for a better offer.

JAZZ BRAIN:

Listen for Inspiration

Great jazz musicians enhance their live performances by playing with other musicians who inspire them. They are constantly listening to one another in ways that can influence the notes, rhythm, or style they are playing. Those moments of interplay among musicians distinguish great jazz performances from merely good ones.

Likewise, you need to really listen to what you're being told during negotiations in order to find solutions to any conflicts that arise. Often, people negotiating have a script in mind for how it will go. They want to obtain a salary of $X, so they ask for 15 percent more than that and expect to negotiate downward to their desired salary. The firm may then start discussing other dimensions of the offer before making a counteroffer on salary. It is easy to stay fixated on the demand you made rather than listening carefully to what the firm is offering.

In many cases, the success of a negotiation rests on trade-offs among dimensions when each party weighs those dimensions differently. Sometimes you can get exactly what you want on the most important dimensions as long as you're willing to give up something you don't care much about. If you aren't much concerned with your start date, for example, you might be willing to delay it awhile in exchange for more paid time off.

Only by listening to how recruiters talk about the aspects of the offer, though, can you come to realize exactly what your priorities are.

Reaching a Decision

At some point, you need to decide. Is this job the one for you? For now, I'm going to focus on choices when you aren't currently employed, though much of what follows also applies when you have a job and are looking for another. In chapter 9, I take up some other issues that are specific to deciding whether to change jobs.

A big factor in this decision is whether the job meets a significant number of your needs. What is the purpose of your job search in the first place? In chapter 2, I talked about the role of values in selecting the jobs you apply for. Look at those values. Does this job actually align with them? Does it provide what you need—whether that's advancing along a career path, providing resources, or giving you the flexibility to pursue other passions?

One thing to remember is that the context of choice is not quite the same as the context once you start working. You may be lucky enough to have more than one offer in hand. If so, you'll be tempted to compare the jobs with each other. One may offer a higher salary. The other may provide more training or give you a more flexible work schedule. Certainly, comparing the two jobs provides information that can be valuable. But the comparison also biases the information you use.

To see how this can happen, we have to delve a bit deeper into the *structural alignment* process that your cognitive brain uses to make comparisons. Dedre Gentner and I have been doing research on this process since I was a graduate student in her lab, many years ago.

When you compare two items, you start by finding all the commonalities you can between them. Some of those may be specific features that are identical. Both jobs may offer two weeks of paid time off, for example. Others may be dimensions—for instance, both jobs will provide you with a salary, but one may pay you more than the other. Because such differences require a point of commonality—that is, both provide salaries—they are called *alignable differences*. Research suggests that when people make comparisons, they focus on alignable differences, because commonalities between options are not very useful for deciding between them.

However, some elements of one option may have no correspondence in the other. For example, one job may offer funding for continuing education, while the other does not. Elements that are unique to one item are called *nonalignable differences*. Studies demonstrate that comparisons de-emphasize nonalignable differences. That means you may discount a property unique to one of the options at the time you make the choice, even though that property may become important later.

So rather than just comparing the options, focus on them individually. Imagine yourself working at each company. Think back on your experiences with the firm, such as your interview or a visit to the corporate headquarters. That will help you imagine actually being in that job.

Of course, even if you notice a nonalignable difference, you may still discount it, because you're not sure how to evaluate it. Is $2,000 in continuing education benefits good or bad? If it was alignable with another offer, that would be easier to determine. After all, a $5,000 benefit is clearly better than a $2,000 one. You need a little more expertise to determine the real value of nonalignable aspects of an offer. That is another place where it may be useful to have an expert to help you.

Reasons and Reactions

As you consider your options, you're likely to engage both your intuitive cognitive brain and your more deliberative cognitive brain. Daniel Kahneman popularized terminology first used by Keith Stanovich and Richard West, who called the intuitive cognitive brain System 1 and the deliberative cognitive brain System 2.

People have a tendency to focus on the deliberative system for making choices. Many studies show that they often select a particular option because it's easy to justify the choice. And the many reasons you generate to make a career choice certainly are important. You should pay attention to all the reasons for and against each option you have.

At the same time, your feelings matter, too. Research by Tim Wilson and colleagues suggests that the emotional reactions you have to options often integrate more information than do the reasons you generate. A good reason is compact and easy to state, but your emotions cut across many different facets of a choice. In addition, reasons tend to focus on things that are easy to talk about, such as salary, benefits, and vacation. Your emotional reactions can be hard to put into words. If you get a tour of the office, you may get a good or a bad vibe from it. Perhaps you're reacting to tension among the employees in a way that would be hard to describe. You have a bad feeling, but you don't know why.

Don't discount such reactions. If you have some concerns about a particular company, try to get more information to help you understand them. Talk to employees. Read reviews on employment websites from current and former employees. I cohost a weekly radio show and podcast called *Two Guys on Your Head* with Bob Duke. Bob is fond of saying that a good decision should think right and feel right. There's a lot of wisdom there. If the reasons you have for a choice and your emotional reactions are misaligned, try to figure out why before moving forward.

Spreading Coherence

As you start leaning toward a particular choice, two factors influence your inclination. First, you engage in motivated reasoning. That is, your motivational brain starts to interpret information in a way that is consistent with the outcome you want. You understand potentially ambiguous information in a way that fits with what you desire. If you hear various rumors about the companies you're considering, you're more likely to believe the ones that are consistent with your desired outcome.

Second, as research on decision making by Jay Russo and colleagues has demonstrated, your cognitive brain shifts attention toward information that is consistent with your current preferences and away from both negative aspects of your desired choice and positive aspects of competing choices. As a result, the desired outcome appears even better than it actually is. This mechanism creates a *spreading coherence* of beliefs. Over time, people come to view their preference as their only possible choice.

It's important to be aware that this is happening, particularly if you do receive some negative information about an employer you're considering. You might be tempted to discount it.

To ensure that you take information that conflicts with your growing inclination into account, systematically document information about your options. If you visit a prospective employer, don't then rely on your memory—take notes immediately after the experience about your impressions and any specific information you got from recruiters or current employees. Similarly, keep notes on your interview and other contacts with recruiters. Retain all your emails from people at the firm and read them over in the course of making your decision.

The spreading coherence of a choice has an impact primarily on your memory and attention. External aids such as lists and emails can ensure that you don't forget key pieces of information as you go along.

Don't Look Back

Once you've made a choice, you have a path. Forge ahead.

You may be tempted to keep comparing your choice with others that you rejected. Little is to be gained from this exercise. Undoubtedly you passed up some good things by rejecting other options in favor of the one you picked. But your career success is now tied to this option.

Even if you have misgivings about your choice, don't let them demotivate you. Your ability to impress the people you work with starts with your commitment to the firm and its mission. So once you make your choice, embrace it fully. You aren't married to this job or this company forever, but you are tied to it for now. In part 2, I will talk about some of the key drivers of success in your job.

Saying No

You may be lucky enough to have more than one option. In that case, you're going to have to disappoint someone by turning them down. When letting a prospective employer know you won't be accepting a job, keep two things in mind.

First, try not to let the difficulty of declining an offer affect your decision. Your motivational brain can kick into avoidance mode when faced with actions you resist. If a prospective employer has been very nice to you, you may feel bad about turning down the offer. As I will discuss in more detail in chapter 6, it's hard in general to deliver bad news. The job you're thinking of turning down may become more appealing. After all, if you can find a reason to say yes, you won't have to contact the firm to say no.

This is when you need to take the long view of the work relationships you're developing. Prospective employers know that they're competing for your services. Whereas you may not say no to a lot of jobs during your lifetime, recruiters are turned down all the time. They generally don't take it personally. (If they do, you probably don't want to work at their company, because they're putting their own goals well ahead of yours.) You need to make the best decision for your career, independent of the desires of the firm recruiting you.

Second, as with other aspects of the job recruitment process, the way you decline an offer will affect your social network. Your aim is to say no to a particular job offer while maintaining a positive reputation with the firm.

If you've developed a personal relationship with the recruiters, turn down the job in a phone call rather than in an email. You may find the social distance provided by an email appealing, but you should make a direct connection. Thank the recruiters for their time and interest. If the decision was hard for you to make, say so. You're likely to encounter people from this company again throughout your career. You may even want a job there someday. Maintaining a cordial relationship will keep the door open for the future.

THE TAKEAWAYS

Your Brains

Motivational Brain

- The strength of your emotional reaction is related to the strength of your engagement with a goal.
- You have a motivational thinking mode and a motivational doing mode.
- Your desired outcome influences the weight you give to new information.

Social Brain

- There is an *information asymmetry* in negotiation. The firm knows a lot of things you don't.
- It can be uncomfortable to say no to other people.

Cognitive Brain

- *Construal level theory* says that the further you are from something in time, space, or social distance, the more abstractly you think about it.
- Metaphors shape the way we think about things.

- Structural alignment focuses you on the *alignable differences* between options rather than the *nonalignable differences*. Non-alignable differences are also harder to evaluate than alignable differences—even when you notice them.

- *Anchoring and adjustment* is a decision strategy whereby you anchor on a number and then adjust away from it toward the desired number. People often adjust insufficiently.

- Your cognitive brain has an intuitive aspect (System 1) and a deliberative aspect (System 2).

Your Tips

- Don't act immediately after learning that you didn't get a job you wanted. Give yourself time to cool off.

- If you don't get a job, feel free to ask recruiters what you could have done better.

- Ask a lot of questions and do a lot of research to prepare for a negotiation. Ask people who work for (or have worked for) the firm for information to reduce the information asymmetry.

- Be prepared to negotiate on all the elements that matter to you.

- Treat negotiations as joint problem-solving exercises rather than competitions.

- Be aware of numbers in the negotiation environment that may serve as anchors; don't let your BATNA serve as one.

- You can learn a lot about a firm by the way it negotiates with you.

- Manipulate the thinking and doing modes in negotiation. Stay in the thinking mode when you don't have a favorable agreement. Push to the doing mode when you're happy with the state of the agreement.

- Good decisions should think right and feel right.

- Don't simply compare prospective options with each other; that will focus you on alignable differences only.

- Be careful not to overweight the positives and underweight the negatives of your desired outcome.

- Don't make job decisions to avoid disappointing a recruiter.

- Turn down job offers personally rather than by email when you have a relationship with the recruiter or the firm.

PART TWO

Succeeding at Work

5

Learning

I n part 2, the focus shifts to doing your job as well as possible. Four central determinants of success are learning, communicating, producing, and leading. I start with learning.

Learning on the job is probably the single most important factor driving your performance at work. You won't know everything you need to about your job when you're hired, no matter how good your education is or how much experience you had in previous positions. The road to learning starts with a willingness to admit what you don't know and an interest in learning new things.

Learning as Gap Filling

Your cognitive brain is the repository for the knowledge you need to do your job well. Three crucial types of knowledge allow you to answer the questions Who? How? and Why? *Who?* refers to the people you must connect with to get the resources, information, assistance, and approval to do your work. (I'll return to this issue later in the chapter when I talk about mentoring.) *How?* refers to the procedures that let you get things done at work. *Why?* involves having good *causal knowledge* about the way the world works within your domain of expertise. With causal knowledge you can solve new problems in new ways rather than just executing a procedure you've learned.

For an example of causal knowledge in action, think about different modes of customer service. Many tech firms have a first line of customer-service representatives at call centers who don't really understand the domain. They work from a script. Because they don't know how the system they're assisting with actually works, they cannot deviate from the script. That's fine if the caller's problem was foreseen in the script, but otherwise, it can lead to a long interaction that fails to resolve the problem. In contrast, a trained expert can diagnose and fix a variety of problems, including those that haven't been encountered before. That's the power of causal understanding.

To improve your expertise, you must first identify gaps in your knowledge. You aren't likely to be motivated to learn new things—nor can you be strategic about learning—if you're not aware of what you do and don't know. Without a good map of the existing state of your knowledge, you'll bump into crucial new knowledge only by chance.

In this section, I explore barriers to finding the gaps in your knowledge. Some of them reside in your cognitive brain—you don't always know what you don't know. Some of them are a facet of your social brain—you aren't always willing to admit what you don't know. I also examine what motivates people to improve their knowledge.

What Don't You Know?

The ability to know what you know and what you don't know is called *metacognition*—that is, the process of thinking about your thinking. Your cognitive brain has a sophisticated ability to assess what you do and don't know. You use several sources of information to make this judgment. Research by Roddy Roediger and Kathleen McDermott identified two significant sources of your judgments about whether you know something: memory and familiarity. If I ask you whether you've heard of Stephen Hawking, you start by trying to pull information about him from your memory. If you recall explicitly that he was a famous physicist or that he worked on black holes and had ALS, then you can judge that you've heard of him.

Of course, you don't always make judgments about what you know by retrieving information. Sometimes you do it according to whether the information feels familiar. If I ask you whether you've heard of Grace Hopper, you may be unable to retrieve any information about her, but her name sounds familiar, so you say you've heard of her. Grace Hopper was a pioneer in computer science who is credited with inventing the term *bug* to refer to errors in a program, but you may judge that you have heard of her even if you don't explicitly remember hearing any information about her. These aspects of metacognition are fine for many types of knowledge. You're pretty good at judging whether you've heard of a particular person or a simple fact. You have a reasonably accurate sense of whether you can perform various procedures. If someone asks you whether you know how to play the piano, your answer is likely to be accurate.

Although your metacognition is good, it isn't perfect. Most people are at least a little overconfident in some areas—particularly when it comes to assessing their proficiency at a task. This overconfidence has sometimes been called the *Lake Wobegon effect*, after the fictional town created by Garrison Keillor for the radio show *Prairie Home Companion*. In Lake Wobegon, "all the women are strong, all the men are good-looking, and all the children are above average."

Research on this topic by David Dunning and Justin Kruger has found that the least skilled people in many domains tend to be the most overconfident in their abilities. One big reason for this is that they don't really understand what expert performance looks like, so they overestimate their own abilities relative to other people's. As you gain expertise, you not only learn new things, but also learn a lot about what you don't yet know.

One important social aspect of the Dunning-Kruger effect is that it often leads to tension between younger employees and the firms they work for. People who don't really understand what skills are required for success in a particular domain may overestimate their own abilities and minimize their perception of the gap between themselves and more-senior members of a firm. As a result, they won't understand why they aren't being promoted faster and will quickly get frustrated in the early stages of their career. The more you appreciate everything involved in expert performance, the more patient you can be with your own development.

A second limitation in your metacognitive abilities is demonstrated in research by Leonid Rosenblit and Frank Keil showing that people overestimate the quality of their causal knowledge. They believe they understand how the world works better than they actually do. The researchers call this miscalibration the *illusion of explanatory depth*.

This illusion has many sources. First, people often use words— particularly in business contexts—whose meaning they don't really understand. When I was writing this book, I heard a lot of people talking about the importance of concepts such as *deep learning* and *blockchain* for the future of business. It wasn't clear that the people using these terms knew much about them. But as a term becomes more familiar, you may feel you understand it even though you don't really.

Causal knowledge has an interesting structure. Unlike stories, which are typically linear, it is nested like Russian dolls. For example, this book is about applying psychology in the workplace, so I use terms drawn from cognitive, social, and motivational psychology. Beneath the level of psychology is neuroscience, which examines brain mechanisms. As I discussed in chapter 1, I'm not really delving deeply into how the brain does what it does, but an understanding of psychology requires some knowledge of the brain. And of course, the nesting continues: unpacking how brain cells work requires a lot of neurochemistry to understand how they generate the electrical signals that carry information.

When you decide whether you understand how something works, you do the mental equivalent of checking whether you have the largest of the Russian dolls—the beginning of a causal explanation. You don't necessarily unpack the explanation completely, though, so you may not realize that after a certain point, one of your dolls is empty. That keeps you from recognizing when you lack key causal knowledge.

You cannot work to fill gaps in your knowledge if you don't know they exist. Research by Michelene Chi and Kurt VanLehn demonstrates that the best way to find such gaps is to explain things to yourself. That is, whenever you encounter a description of how something works, you should explain it back to yourself to determine what you've actually learned. That is the mental equivalent of opening the Russian dolls in your mind to make sure that you have the complete set.

This process can help you learn what you do and don't know. Whether you choose to fill the gaps is up to you. I'll pick up later on how to decide what gaps you want to fill.

Admitting Gaps and Mistakes

There are many ways to fill gaps in your knowledge. A common one is to search the internet. You've probably visited a number of websites that suggest sources of information about a variety of topics. Even a cursory internet search will turn up a lot of videos that show you how to carry out particular tasks.

The most powerful source of knowledge is the people around you. Your colleagues—and particularly your supervisor—should be helping you develop your career. They know how things work at your company. They have developed expertise in solving many of the problems you'll face on a daily basis. They are also likely to have suggestions for how to learn relevant information about your job.

To engage your colleagues to help you learn, you need to overcome a few barriers erected by your social brain.

The first is that if you're like most other people, you resist admitting ignorance to save face in social situations. It's potentially embarrassing to own up that you don't know something. This effect is so powerful that it occurs even in anonymous surveys—people will select a middle option in a range to communicate that they don't know enough to have an opinion.

Sometimes people don't want to admit ignorance because they suffer from *imposter syndrome*. That is, they believe that they are frauds who have risen to a position they don't deserve. Women are more likely than men to hold this attitude. Imposter syndrome makes people less likely either to admit what they don't know or to own mistakes they've made. After all, if you fear that you don't actually deserve to be in a position, you expect that a lack of knowledge or an error will be taken as confirming evidence. As a result, you won't reach out to others to get the help you need, and your work performance will suffer, reinforcing your belief that you're in over your head. Imposter syndrome becomes a self-fulfilling prophecy.

Many people are reluctant to admit mistakes in the workplace. You've probably been socialized to think mistakes are bad. Your success in school, from kindergarten to the end of your education, depended largely on finding ways to minimize the number of your mistakes. Getting good grades on tests required making as few errors as possible. If you believe that mistakes are bad, you won't want to advertise them—or the gaps in your knowledge—to others.

Furthermore, because people fear they will be punished for making mistakes, they want to keep them secret. It's a common cultural norm that "someone must be held accountable" for a mistake. And people should certainly be punished for negligent actions. But legitimate errors are learning experiences, even when they have significant consequences.

As it happens, admitting a mistake is one of the best ways to gain the trust of your boss. I opened this book with a story about my son who approached his boss after a bad interaction with a client in his first job. His boss immediately gave him some good suggestions about how to deal with that client in the future and thanked him for coming to see her. He continued to get more opportunities at the company.

If you admit mistakes, your managers will learn that you'll come to them when you don't know something or when a problem arises. As a result, they'll be more likely to trust you with new assignments. I'll return to this idea when discussing leadership in chapter 8.

The key lesson here is that you must overcome the many forces in your social brain that want you to keep secret your mistakes and the gaps in your knowledge. Only when you reveal what you need to learn can you be taught by your more knowledgeable colleagues.

Motivation to Learn and the Expert Generalist

Once you've identified gaps in your knowledge, you must decide what you actually need to learn. People typically focus on acquiring information that is most directly relevant to the job they've taken on. That's a good strategy at first. Chances are, your new job requires you to do a number of things you've never done before or to do them faster, more efficiently, and more effectively than in the past. You want to focus on excelling at your new responsibilities.

After you get the hang of a new position, be strategic about what you learn. You probably need a wider range of expertise than you think. Solving hard problems at work requires drawing not just on expertise from within the domain of your work, but also on knowledge about other areas that may not have seemed relevant at first. The history of invention is filled with examples of people who drew on unexpected sources of knowledge. George de Mestral invented Velcro after examining the cockleburs that stuck so persistently to his dog's fur. James Dyson's insight for his vacuum came from knowledge of sawmills and industrial cyclones. Fiona Fairhurst led a team at Speedo that used the structure of sharkskin to design the material for a swimsuit.

The trade-off is that every day you probably have a long list of jobs you're expected to complete. Where can you find the time to learn things that aren't directly related to them? And without learning about a variety of new things, how can you help your organization find new solutions to problems?

One group of people has resolved this trade-off in an interesting way: expert generalists. As I wrote in my book *Habits of Leadership*, expert generalists have a lot of knowledge on a wide variety of topics. As a result, they are often involved in innovative projects. Indeed, I first identified the characteristics of expert generalists by studying Victor Mills Society Fellows at Procter & Gamble. Individuals at P&G are given this designation (named after the man behind Pampers) because they are good serial innovators.

Expert generalists have several motivational personality traits. They are very open to experience (interested in new things). They are high in need for cognition (not one of the big five personality traits, but important for the workplace), which reflects how much someone likes to think deeply about things. People high in this quality often continue to research new topics they encounter. The combination of high openness to experience and high need for cognition ensures that expert generalists learn deeply about a number of topics.

At the same time, they are often moderate to low in conscientiousness (which *is* a big five trait). Conscientiousness leads people to finish the tasks they start—and also to follow the rules. Individuals with low conscientiousness are willing to put aside some of their assigned work to pursue knowledge by reading articles, watching videos, and talking with other people.

Unfortunately, people are often rewarded for conscientiousness early in their careers. That's why many of the innovators I encountered talked about succeeding "despite the system, not because of it." Their supervisors would often call them out for not completing their assigned work without recognizing that what they did instead may have been time well spent. As a result, these supervisors were unwittingly putting pressure on their team to constrain how much they learned.

Regardless of your level of conscientiousness, you almost always have some latitude to craft aspects of your job that are important to you. You should ask for time on a regular basis to pursue interesting ideas, even if you aren't immediately sure how they relate to your job. Any employer that is serious about innovation should be willing to free you to improve the breadth and quality of your knowledge.

Mentors

Julius Caesar said that experience is the best teacher. He was right that in the grand scheme of things we learn from, experience is powerful. But Benjamin Franklin was also on to something when he said, "Experience keeps a dear school, but fools will learn in no other."

The best teachers may be the people around you.

A remarkable source of your ability to adapt to the world is that you can learn about almost anything if you want to. But you don't always know what you need to know to succeed. That's where colleagues can be helpful. If you want to excel at work, you'll need mentors.

Many organizations recognize the importance of mentorship to employee success, so they have mentorship programs in place. Soon after being hired, you may be contacted by someone who, you are told, is your mentor. The two of you may go out once for coffee or lunch and talk—and you may never really talk to that person again.

A mentorship program like that fails, because it is *inorganic*. When you first start working for an organization, you may not know what you need to succeed. And a mentor who is handed to you won't know your goals, your strengths, and your weaknesses. Such mentors often give bland and generic advice.

The trick is to approach mentorship more organically. As you get to know your workplace, you will naturally meet some people with skills and abilities you'd like to have. Those are the people you should get to know. Approach them and ask for a little of their time to learn about the source of their success. People usually find it flattering to be seen as having a skill you want to develop and are generally quite willing to pass along what they know.

When you meet with a mentor, don't just sit, listen, and take notes. Talk frankly about the aspects of your work that you want to improve. The more your mentors know about you, the better the advice they can give. Ask them to give you an assignment—something to read, something to do. Learning is an active process and requires effort on your part.

The people you choose as mentors are usually important people in the organization. They may have leadership roles and some opportunity to influence your future. If you call on such people for their expertise, make sure you follow up on their suggestions. If they highly recommend a book, read it. If they suggest you develop a skill, work on it. Once you've made yourself visible, impress the mentor with your effort.

The Lineup of Your Mentoring Team

A second problem with mentoring programs at many organizations is that they assign a single mentor to an employee. Rarely can one individual address all the ways that you'd like to see your career grow. Concentrate on developing a team of mentors who can guide you through your career, and consider several types of mentorship.

One important member of your team is a *coach*. A good coach may or may not be a superstar at work but really knows the workplace and has a lot of experience. This person should be able to help you identify your strengths and weaknesses. Coaches play two important roles for you. They listen to your description of a problem you're facing, ask you questions that might help you see it differently, and guide you toward a solution so that you'll be able to handle similar things in the future. And they suggest how you can improve your performance at work, whether by reading certain books, joining certain groups, or acquiring new skills.

There is a big and important difference between a coach and an adviser. Advisers listen to what you have to say and then recommend a course of action. It's tempting to seek them, because they provide an easy way to solve problems. But ultimately you have to find solutions on your own. That means you need someone to walk you through the process of figuring out what to do in a new situation rather than just telling you what to do.

Another good mentor is a *superstar*. You're bound to know a few people in the workplace (or in your broader social network) who are truly successful. They have what you want. Connect with these people. Take them out for a cup of coffee. Send them an occasional email. You want to get nuggets from them on how they reached their peak. These people may not have a ton of time to spend with you, but whatever time you get with them is likely to be valuable. You may think that a real superstar doesn't want to talk to you. But many successful people had mentors of their own who helped them out early in their careers. Besides, most people are flattered when you want them to talk about themselves.

Your mentorship team also needs a good *connector*. To accomplish your goals, you'll often need the help of other people—particularly people who have the skills to get jobs completed. You should find out who controls the resources you'll need when starting a project.

Occasionally, you can find the person you're looking for through LinkedIn or other social media, but you might be looking for a needle in a haystack. And cold-contacting someone on social media is not always successful.

A connector is someone with a wide social network who is skilled at greasing the gears of the social engine. When you approach connectors with a problem you're trying to solve, they often know several people who would be valuable for you to talk to and are willing to introduce you to those people to get things started. A connector can help you with the *Who?* question mentioned earlier in this chapter.

The next person to look for is someone I call a *librarian.* This person is particularly valuable in a large organization where you're unfamiliar with all the resources available. If you work for a small firm, you know everyone by name and have a clear sense of their responsibilities. In large organizations, though, it can be hard to know what office, group, or person you need to get things done. And you may not understand why particular policies have been put in place. A librarian can help you navigate these complexities and allow you to take full advantage of what your organization has to offer. Sometimes that librarian is a staff member or admin who has been with the organization for a long time and knows all of its deep dark secrets.

It's also valuable to have a good *teammate* as a mentor—someone who understands what you're going through at work, will let you vent when you need to, and can lend a sympathetic ear when you've had a tough day. You don't want to air every grievance with everyone at work, but having one or two trusted confidants is important. They need not work in your organization, but they should know enough about your work that you don't have to explain everything from the beginning.

Your mentoring team doesn't necessarily have to be stable. Just keep a group of people in your orbit to whom you can reach out regularly for help. Some people may drift out of your sphere, and others may gravitate into it. Try to keep up with all your mentors, though, to maintain a good working relationship with them.

The Value of Being a Mentor

Not only should you learn from your colleagues, but you should strive to share what you know as widely as possible. Mentoring others has several benefits.

I mentioned earlier in this chapter that the best cure for the illusion of explanatory depth is to explain something you've learned. Ideally, you'll get in the habit of explaining things to yourself. Mentoring provides you with an opportunity to explain things to others. Working with other people can broaden your own understanding of some key aspect of the work you do.

Carine told me that she enjoys taking new employees at her firm out for coffee when they first arrive and answering any questions they might have. One newcomer asked her about the reason behind a safety policy for the factory floor that seemed antiquated given the available technology. In trying to explain the policy, Carine realized that she had no idea why it had been established. After researching the history, she got a small working group together to revise it. She commented that it's often valuable to see things at the company with fresh eyes.

Your social network at an organization tends to solidify quickly. In your first few months at work, you meet a lot of people. Then, as you settle into a routine, you connect with fewer new individuals and rely on the ones you know to help you with projects. That can create cliques or mini-silos within your organization. Mentoring others is a great and low-cost way to expand your network. You'll get to know not only your mentees, but also some of the people they're connected with.

Another important benefit comes as you get further along in your career. When you start out, you're often excited about your prospects. You are embarking on a new adventure. As time goes by, though, even if you believe deeply in your organization's mission and that your contribution is valuable, you may lose the enthusiasm you had when you began.

Your mentees are typically earlier in their journey. They may be new to the organization, or they may be taking on a new role. Either way, they're focused on the future and bring energy to their jobs. Through the mechanisms of goal contagion, that energy is infectious. By spending time with people who are excited about pursuing a new goal, you can reinvigorate yourself and often find renewed purpose in your own work.

JAZZ BRAIN:

Playing with Your Head and Your Heart

I've heard jazz players talk about the difference between "head" players and "heart" players. Head players know their music theory in and out and focus on playing solos that fit technically. Heart players listen to what other musicians are doing and play what feels right in the situation. They may not be the most theoretically savvy musicians, but they find ways to sound good.

Truly great players play with both head and heart—they put in the time to internalize a lot of music theory and then use that theory in the service of listening and playing. It sounds easy, but it isn't.

The best people in the workplace also play with their heads and their hearts. They become real experts in their domain. But they're comfortable enough with their knowledge to be able to listen and to adapt what they know to the circumstances. It's a matter of learning when the textbook response is the right one and when to deviate.

The best way to get there is to keep developing both your base of knowledge and your ability to pay attention to the situation. Chances are, one of your superstar mentors plays with both head and heart. Watch that person and strive to follow his or her lead.

Continuing Education

Continual learning is crucial for a successful career. The skills and knowledge you have on day one will help you get started, but the job you'll have even a few years from now will require new skills and knowledge. You won't gain them just in the course of your daily work. Continual learning is often aimed at filling gaps or purposefully building new capabilities—as opposed to the kind of learning that expert generalists do, the purpose of which may not be obvious in advance.

Talk with your mentoring team about the knowledge and skills you don't yet have that will enable you to achieve your goals. Of course, for that conversation to be productive, you'll need to think more about your trajectory. I'll take up that topic in more detail in chapter 9.

A natural way to acquire additional knowledge is on your own. The web pages of most business magazines are now stocked with blogs exploring topics that might suggest new ways to think about work. Countless YouTube videos are how-to guides for skills ranging from using spreadsheets to programming. Work-related podcasts also provide an interesting source of material. And many books out there (like this one) are aimed at getting you to think differently about your work skills.

Often it's easy to access these sources of information during downtimes in your schedule. Podcasts and audiobooks make good companions during your daily commute or when you have to travel for work. Videos and blogs are handy when you find yourself between tasks or needing a change of pace. You can leave a book in a convenient place at home to pick up when you have a little extra time. The main thing is to develop the habit of trying to learn something new.

The internet hasn't made more-structured training obsolete, though. Some things are hard to learn on your own. One of my graduate mentors, Doug Medin, suggests focusing coursework on skills that you wouldn't be able to learn easily by just reading a book. In my field, that includes statistical analysis, qualitative methods, and computer programming. Those skills are best learned when a structured curriculum leads you through the core concepts and instructors guide you through the assignments and evaluate your work.

You have several options for finding courses to learn new skills.

As mentioned earlier, many organizations offer internal training opportunities. Some of these are provided regularly to every employee, but others require some initiative on your part. If your company has an internal website that lists training programs, check it regularly for sessions that would enhance your capabilities. A training session may take you away from your regular work for a day or two, but it will pay significant dividends down the line.

A great example of this kind of program comes from USAA, a firm that provides financial services to active-duty military personnel, veterans, and their families. The company has a commitment to innovation, so it has developed an innovator certification program in collaboration with the IC^2 Institute at the University of Texas. People accepted into this program get a semester of training on how to develop new ideas, evaluate them, and test their market effectiveness. Graduates of the program then work across the company to nurture new ideas.

Also find out whether your company will support professional training by outside organizations. Many universities and groups have seminars that are offered on an ongoing basis to provide workplace skills. These seminars often last for one or two days, and you may have the option of taking several seminars over time to earn a certificate related to a key workplace skill. These programs expose you to the thinking of cutting-edge researchers and to tools derived from new research. They are well worth exploring, even if you have to pay out of pocket.

Mel, who directs training for a large consulting firm, said that her organization offers $5,000 a year per employee for outside classes, yet few take advantage of those funds. To ensure you don't miss out on these opportunities, get recommendations for organizations that run seminars in your area. Check out the schedule of classes early in the fiscal year and put the seminars on your calendar before major projects come up. You're much more likely to follow through on training if you build it into your schedule in advance than if you wait for the unlikely event of a lull.

You might also look outside your organization to get an advanced degree. A master's or even a doctorate may help propel you into the next stage of your career. Advanced degree programs are time-consuming and can be expensive, but they can also be transformative if they equip you to pursue your work in a new way. One thing you might want to do early in your career is look at the educational background of people who have jobs you think you might want someday. If many of them have advanced degrees, think about how a degree program might fit into your life. You don't necessarily have to get the particular degree your colleagues have earned, but knowing that some degree program is in your future can help you plan to make that happen.

And while we're on the topic of degree programs, let me make a pitch for working parents to consider continuing their education. I have run a master's program for working professionals for six years. I also raised kids of my own. I know how hard it is to juggle work and home life. And if you have young children, life is a constant blur of activity. As your kids get older, though, they are paying attention to what you do by way of thinking about what their future might look like. When they see you working toward an advanced degree, it sends a message about the importance of education that goes far beyond anything you might say to them. You may think that the time you devote to your education takes away from quality time with your children, but a few hours working side by side with them on homework could be some of the best time you ever spend.

THE TAKEAWAYS

Your Brains

Motivational Brain

- Need for cognition is a trait that reflects how much people like to think about things.

- Conscientiousness is a trait that reflects how much people want to finish what they start.

Social Brain

- A lot of what you learn comes from the people around you.

- You can be energized by observing the action and enthusiasm of others.

Cognitive Brain

- Causal knowledge allows you to answer new questions in new ways. Your causal knowledge has a nested structure.

- Metacognition is your ability to reflect on your own thinking. You may know you know something because you remember it explicitly or just because you have a feeling that you know it.

- The Dunning-Kruger effect says that the least skilled people are the least aware of how much they know.

- People suffer from an *illusion of explanatory depth*, whereby they believe they understand the way the world works better than they actually do.

Your Tips

- Don't be afraid to admit what you don't know.

- Be the first to confess your mistakes.

- You need to know more than you think you do.

- Expert generalists are valuable in innovation settings.
- Think carefully about who you want on your mentoring team and seek those people out.
- Mentoring others has great value.
- Learn to act in the workplace with your head *and* your heart.
- Look for opportunities for continuing education—both formal and informal.

6

Communicating

One thing that distinguishes humans from the other species on Earth is our ability to communicate in a variety of ways. Most animals communicate with other members of their species—and sometimes with potential predators or prey. They have mechanisms to attract mates, warn potential enemies, or signal danger. They may communicate through sounds, movements, or even chemical trails.

But humans have a complex language that allows us to add new words at will to name objects, actions, and concepts as our information environment changes. We are skilled at metaphor and analogy, permitting us to extend the meanings of words to cover new situations. We have developed a variety of technologies for communicating with one another even when we aren't in the same place at the same time. Indeed, this book allows me to share my knowledge with you across time and space.

Language is central to human nature. We learn our native language just by being born into a particular culture. If it's an environment in which multiple languages are spoken, we learn them all and use them in different contexts. Despite the importance of language to everything we do, we recognize that not everyone is a good communicator.

Some people are more skilled at conveying information clearly or using language to motivate others.

To succeed in the workplace, you must master the art of sharing information across a variety of modalities, including email, text, writing, and speech. In this chapter, I explore some key aspects of communication and look at ways to recognize your weaknesses and to improve as a communicator.

What Is Communication?

People's ability to communicate with one another evolved in an environment in which small numbers of native speakers of the same language spoke face-to-face in real time. As the psycholinguist Herb Clark points out, the further we get from this ideal, the harder it is to communicate effectively.

Advances in technology allow you to communicate with people from around the globe who grew up speaking different languages. You can be far away and unable to see your conversation partners. You can communicate across time through writing—in which case your conversation partners cannot hear you or respond immediately to what you've said. Each deviation from the ideal creates opportunities for miscommunication.

The ideal form of communication works so well because it facilitates a coordinated effort between speaker and hearer. You may think that the way conversation works is that a speaker has an idea and translates it into sentences. The hearer deconstructs those sentences into the ideas the speaker presumably intended and then formulates a message to be sent back to the speaker.

At an abstract level, this sounds reasonable. Certainly, when you read dialogue in a novel, conversations play out that way. But real dialogues are much more complicated. For one thing, the hearer plays an active part in the conversation. To see the truth of that, notice what you're doing next time you're in a conversation and someone else is talking. By looking at the speaker, you communicate that you're paying attention to what is being said. Nodding indicates that you understand and generally agree with it. If you suddenly have something to say, you may change your posture to signal that you'd like a turn in the conversation.

Speakers are usually sensitive to what hearers are doing. If you're talking and your conversation partner suddenly looks quizzical or angry, you stop to figure out what's wrong. You try to repair misunderstandings as quickly as possible to ensure that the conversation doesn't get derailed.

The way you talk also takes into account a lot of the knowledge that you believe you share with your conversation partner. In general, your speech obeys the *given-new* convention. That is, you refer to something you assume the hearer will understand and then provide a new piece of information that adds to their knowledge. If you say, "Raul is now manager of the marketing team," you assume that your conversation partner knows who Raul is but not that he has been promoted. If you misestimate the knowledge of your conversation partners, you're likely to confuse them by referring to things they don't know or bore them by providing information they already have.

Another aspect of language to consider is that we don't say everything we want to say directly. We regularly use many conventions that we expect other people to understand. For example, the most direct way to get someone to do something for you is to issue a command, such as "Make these copies for me." But that can sound harsh to native speakers of English in the United States, so we often phrase a request as a question: "Would you make these copies for me?" The intent is still a directive; you don't expect the person to say no. But you're acknowledging their ability to act as they choose by stating your request indirectly.

These are just a few of the many things that can cause your conversations to fail. In this chapter, I explore a few common communication problems and talk about how to avoid them.

Communicating Effectively in Different Modes

Perhaps the most important point of this brief overview of communication is that its ideal form is one that we engage in less and less often in the workplace. For a number of reasons, much of our face-to-face communication has been replaced by emails, texts, and instant messages punctuated with the occasional phone call or video conference. Some small conversations and group meetings still occur, but they're no longer the most frequent way of passing on information.

To be a good communicator, you must know the limitations of the modes you're using so that you can minimize potential problems. Thinking through these limitations may lead you to shift your strategy away from some modes and toward others—at least in some circumstances. I'll start with a discussion of text-based communication and then turn to phone and video conferencing (such as Skype). In the next section, I'll focus on meetings.

Text Communication

In many organizations, you have several options for text-based communications. You probably get a lot of emails each day. Some are addressed directly to you, some are group discussions, and some are memos and newsletters circulated to a very large number of people (spam). You may have a text messaging system on your phone or an instant messaging system on a device that you're expected to monitor and use. You may be part of a social network or message-board site or app where articles and discussions are posted for comment.

Three communication problems can arise when you communicate too often with text. First, asking for clarification by email can be difficult, leading to miscommunication. Second, whatever back-and-forth is necessary to clarify something may actually take more time via text than in person. Third, establishing the right tone can be challenging, making it hard to maintain relationships. Email and instant messages can also be a source of distraction—I'll return to that issue in chapter 7.

Another problem with text is that you may misestimate the knowledge you share with someone else. You might use an unfamiliar word or jargon term. You might refer to things the other person doesn't know about in ways that cause confusion. Rajesh told me about an email in which a colleague asked him to look at "the report" and fix any errors. Unfortunately, the report that Rajesh thought his colleague was referring to was a different one. As a result, he spent a morning working on something his colleague wasn't interested in.

You might think that Rajesh could have asked for clarification up front. But he was relatively sure he knew which report was meant. And even if he had some reservations, sending an email could have delayed the process significantly, because Rajesh was in India, while his colleague was in New York. Rather than take the time to clarify, he forged ahead.

In face-to-face communication, we often negotiate meanings. Consider this unremarkable snippet of dialogue:

A: Have you heard from Sydney?

B: Sydney from marketing?

A: No, our office in Australia.

B: Ah, not yet. I'm expecting an email from them tonight.

In the span of just moments, an ambiguous word (Sydney) was clarified, and the question was answered. This dialogue would occupy about ten seconds of someone's time during the day unless it happened via email—in which case, a few hours might elapse between messages. And messages can take longer to process if you have to read back through the thread to remember what was going on in the conversation.

In many offices, people have developed the habit of communicating with most of their colleagues using text. It appears easier, because you don't have to interrupt what they're doing—they can check their emails or texts when it's convenient. But that can actually waste a lot of time, particularly when a seemingly simple request requires a number of turns to resolve.

For greater efficiency, try dealing with simple requests either in person or on the phone. We've fallen out of the habit of poking our head in on colleagues or setting up a quick chat. But it's amazing how much time you can save by talking to people in person for small things. And as your colleagues learn that when you say you need a minute of their time, you mean that literally, they become more willing to engage in a quick chat or phone call.

Having more conversations and fewer text interactions can also assist in establishing the right tone. Stacy told me that she had recently started a new job working remotely. Her supervisor said that people in the office had complaints about requests she had made to move projects forward. Stacy had never had friction with colleagues before; she realized that a big part of the problem was that most of her interactions with the rest of the office were by email.

That's not surprising. If you ask someone to make copies for you in person, you can convey how much you appreciate their efforts by the way you phrase the question, your tone of voice, and the look on your face. Text allows you to choose your phrasing, but your tone and facial expression are missing (even when you add emojis to what you write). As a result, a simple "Please make these copies for me" can sound like a command in an email. Over time, you may get a reputation for being demanding or difficult.

In general, spending some time with colleagues is valuable, even if the bulk of your interactions are by text. Face time helps people get to know you better, which makes their evaluations of what you say more charitable. Your social brain reacts better to people you know than to people you don't, so developing relationships with colleagues will smooth your ability to communicate with them by text. When they know you, they can hear your voice behind the text.

Communication at a Distance

Technology also supports real-time communication at a distance. Obviously, the phone lets you talk with people who aren't in the room with you. Video conferencing software like Skype, Google Hangouts, and Zoom supports simultaneous video and audio.

These modes of communication provide a lot more information than text alone does. You can hear someone's tone of voice. You can get information that signals people's interest or excitement. Consider the difference between these two exchanges:

A: Would you join the hiring committee?

B: Sure.

A: Would you join the hiring committee?

B: [Long pause] Sure.

Even if the tone of voice is the same, the pause communicates uncertainty.

With video conferencing tools, you can see the people you're speaking to. Facial expressions can communicate interest, irony, sarcasm, or boredom. Video also permits a shared environment. When people share a computer screen or a slide deck, they are anchoring the discussion in something that everyone in the conversation can see. The cursor lets them point to items in the environment—"this one" or "here."

Where these forms of communication create the most difficulty is in small-group settings such as conference calls. Conversation in a shared environment is a coordinated dance. When one person is speaking, everyone else looks at them. When someone else in the group wants to contribute, they will often call attention to themselves to indicate that. The speaker then looks directly at them and cedes the floor. And when people are in a shared environment, it's easy to see when someone isn't participating and give them an opportunity to do so.

Phone and video conferencing make this process harder. People can't gracefully indicate that they'd like to speak, and handing over the floor is challenging for the speaker. As a result, awkward pauses often occur when someone finishes speaking, or several people jump in at the same time. People who don't tend to participate in group conversations can easily fade into the background—particularly on conference calls, where they have no visual cues.

When you're leading a conference call or a video conference, try to help move the conversation along. Keep track of times when several people start to speak and make sure they all have a chance to contribute before the conversation progresses too far. Keep a list of everyone in attendance and elicit comments from people who haven't said much. Running a conference call or video conference is not like having a group conversation in a common space. You have to more deliberately keep track of who has spoken and be more mindful of the dynamics of the meeting. Things that come naturally when you're working with others in the same space may require more effort.

Meetings

No element of work life is more common or more maligned than meetings. We get together in groups for many reasons, among them to develop new ideas, share plans, solve problems, coordinate projects, and reach consensus. Meetings can be a productive way to get work done, but many times they are not. One problem is that often a few people tend to dominate what's said. A second is that key things may go unsaid. A third is that meetings are frequently not organized around clear goals that can be accomplished by getting a group together.

The Dominator

The Pareto principle states that 80 percent of any outcome typically comes from only 20 percent of the potential causes. This rule may be particularly apt with regard to meetings. It always seems that 80 percent of the comments are made by 20 percent of the attendees.

That happens for several reasons. Not everyone in the meeting has the expertise—the cognitive brain—needed to participate fully on every topic. So some people must necessarily listen to the proceedings rather than contribute.

Two personality characteristics—the motivational brain—drive people to engage in meetings. First, extraversion (another member of the big five) reflects how much people like to be the center of attention in social situations. Extraverts in a meeting enjoy the social give-and-take and are more likely than introverts to speak. Second, narcissism makes some people believe that they're superior to those around them, who ought to pay attention to what they say. Narcissists will speak early and often at meetings but usually don't listen to what others—particularly those who disagree with them—have to say.

Your social brain can help you learn good meeting behavior. If you pay attention to what other people do in meetings, you'll get a sense of how to contribute. Watching the reactions of others as you speak is helpful. If they look attentive, you're probably contributing something of value without going on too long. If they look away or whisper to one another, you're probably saying too much. It's important to speak up when you have something to say (I'll take that up again in the next section), but you want to be sure not to speak more often than everyone else. If you think you might be dominating, try recording a meeting you attend (with permission from the other participants, of course) and listen to your contributions later. Was what you were saying on topic? Did you move the conversation forward? Did you remain concise?

It's hard to speak in sound bites, but that's a valuable skill to learn, because people are likely to remember sound bites and use them throughout the rest of the conversation. A sound bite need not over-simplify the topic, but it should briefly state your main point. Spend some time looking over the meeting agenda in advance and think about some of the key topics. Write down your thoughts ahead of time and see if you can find some clear phrases to use in discussing them.

A key reason people drone on in meetings is that they have something to say but haven't quite figured out how to articulate it. So they take the floor and speak until they figure out a way to phrase their intended point. You frequently have to respond spontaneously in a meeting, choosing the words to express a thought in real time. The more you practice crafting pithy ways to phrase what you're thinking, the better able you'll be to do that in the moment.

Pay attention to how much time you take when you speak in a meeting. If you spend more than a minute on a given turn, you're probably going on too long. If you speak for several minutes, you're probably making several points—so if you want people to respond to the things you're saying, focus on one or perhaps two issues at a time. Otherwise, most of what you say will get lost. Furthermore, if you get a reputation for droning on in meetings, people may tune you out entirely, severely diminishing your impact.

Finally, a cardinal sin in meetings is "me-too-ing," whereby one person makes an important point, and then several other people take the floor to say essentially the same thing (perhaps in other words). Before you raise your hand in a meeting, ask yourself whether you have something new to contribute. If someone offers what appears to be an unpopular opinion with which you agree, you ought to speak in support, but that can be done quickly. Avoid the temptation to take a full turn just to tread the same ground walked on by previous speakers. And be particularly mindful of repeating a point made by someone else without acknowledging who said it first in the meeting. A common observation is that more powerful people will repeat a point made by a less powerful person in the room and ultimately get credit for someone else's idea.

To be an effective communicator in meetings, avoid dominating the proceedings. When you're leading a meeting, keep it flowing, even if you have one or more dominators in the room. At the end of this discussion of meetings, I'll talk about strategies for leading effective ones and explore some ways to tame people who might otherwise take over.

The Things That Go Unsaid

Several years ago, when I was consulting for a large company, I sat in on a two-hour meeting in which an organizational leader facilitated a discussion about a new initiative under development. Many people took turns, and a few friendly amendments were added to the proposal. As we were walking out, I stood behind two midlevel managers. One leaned over to the other and offered several reasons why the plan was misguided. A few of the points he made deserved consideration and discussion. Unfortunately, none of them had been made during the meeting, when they might have influenced consideration of the proposal.

JAZZ BRAIN:

Silence Is a Note

Jazz musicians relish their turn to take a solo. Early on, it's tempting to fill that moment with as many licks and flourishes as possible. But as the great trumpet player Miles Davis said, "It's not the notes you play, it's the notes you don't play."

Similarly, when you're speaking in public or in a meeting, you may tend to fall back on verbal tics to help you hold the floor: "umm" to fill a pause, or "you know" to end a sentence. Such sounds or words may pop out of your mouth automatically, but they quickly become annoying to those listening to you.

If you notice that you're using verbal tics (or if someone points them out to you), you need to practice replacing them with silence. An easy way to do that is to slow down when you're speaking in conversations and meetings. It's hard to control your speech when you talk fast, but if you take your time, you may start to hear the noises you make to fill the silence. And when you speak more slowly, you also tend to enunciate better, making it easier for others to understand everything you say.

When organizations develop new initiatives, their plans are only as good as the collective knowledge of the individuals who work for them. Meetings are one of the ways we attempt to tap that knowledge. But people encounter barriers to speaking up and sharing their expertise.

Some organizations simply don't want dissenting opinions (no matter how much they may say they do). Lena worked for a nonprofit that focuses on public school students. The organization has a strong donor base and a powerful mission. Like any other organization, it had some programs that worked well and some that needed improvement. The leadership was quick to tout the great things it did, and claimed to encourage staff members to suggest programming improvements.

Unfortunately, no action was ever taken on any of Lena's suggestions. She stopped giving feedback and eventually left to work for an organization that was more receptive to her ideas.

You must judge by the actions of the people in management whether they are truly interested in suggestions for making the organization better. When you find yourself in a position of some authority, it's important to listen to people's recommendations and to follow up later to let them know what if any action has been taken.

If you want truly constructive criticism of new ideas, though, it's also important to give people time to think about their concerns prior to a meeting. You can circulate proposals in advance and encourage people to send in comments. You might even offer to create an anonymized list of comments in case some people are concerned that they might get a reputation for being contrary.

Develop strategies for providing your own constructive feedback on proposals. Early on in your tenure at an organization, you may not feel comfortable voicing your views in group meetings. If so, reach out to a trusted colleague or your supervisor to discuss your thoughts. Ask for advice about the most appropriate way within the culture of the organization to provide your comments so that you can become more comfortable making them in a group setting as well as in one-on-one meetings.

Designing Your Meetings Backward

The success of a meeting is crucially determined by its structure. Early in your career, you may not have many opportunities to run meetings of your own. That's a great time to put your social brain to work and watch how the people you admire set up their meetings. In this section, I present a few suggestions for maximizing the value of meetings you run.

The most important thing you can do when setting up a meeting is engage in what educators call *backward design*. Whenever you create an experience for other people—whether it's a course, a lecture, or a meeting—start by thinking about the end goal. What do you want to accomplish? How do you want the participants to be different at the end of the experience from the way they were before it began? Then focus all your efforts on achieving that goal.

The work starts with deciding who should attend the meeting. You need people with expertise that will be relevant to solving any problems that must be addressed. You need stakeholders who may have to approve the results of the meeting. Identify individuals who should stay in the loop on developments related to what will be discussed.

Also, think about who *doesn't* need to be there. The dynamics of a meeting change a lot as it gets larger. When three people are working together, everyone participates. As the number grows, it becomes easier for some people to disappear. By the time ten people are in the room, there's a good chance that several of them will say nothing during the meeting. If twenty or more are there, the meeting is likely to become a series of presentations rather than a dynamic discussion.

Next, construct a clear agenda. Concentrate on discussions and activities that will help achieve the goal. Put together a timeline to ensure that you stay on track and complete the items on the agenda. It's common to spend a lot of time on the first few items and rush through the rest.

I've served on a large university-wide committee whose meetings are regularly attended by many of the top-level administrators. With that much expertise in the room, it would be great to work on important problems facing the institution—and invariably some of those are on the agenda. However, the meeting is often structured to start with a number of summaries of written reports. We frequently don't get to the important discussion topics until just a few minutes before the meeting adjourns. This gathering would be much more effective if we began with the discussion topics and saved the reports for the second half, because attendees could read them over later if there wasn't enough time for oral summaries. Indeed, this committee has recently started circulating reports and skipping the in-person recitation of the information unless there is time after having discussions that take advantage of the talent in the room.

Before the meeting starts, circulate copies of any documents you want people to look at. Remind them a couple of times to review the materials so that the discussion can be productive. Nothing stalls a meeting as much as having to summarize documents for one or two people who came poorly prepared.

When you run meetings, be careful not to dominate. You can give a brief opening statement, but get on to the important agenda items quickly, and let everyone participate. If you know there's a dominator in the meeting, consider ways to ensure that everyone gets a turn. You might go around the room and give everyone a chance to speak, or ask a few people in advance to prepare some things to say.

Finally, when the meeting is over, send everyone a summary of what happened and highlight the key action items. This summary will be particularly helpful if others remember the meeting differently. Invite people to comment on your summary, because they may point out things you missed. You want to help meeting participants engage their motivational brains, so if a particular person needs to follow up on something, send them a reminder soon after the meeting with specific instructions and a date for completion.

If you get a reputation for running good and productive meetings, you'll be noticed and will be given more opportunities to do interesting projects.

Hard Conversations

Even if you're a perfectly clear communicator, there are conversations you don't want to have. For example, in chapter 5, I pointed out that you have to admit what you don't know before you can learn new things. But letting someone else know the limitations of your knowledge and skills can be hard—particularly if you suffer from imposter syndrome.

In general, difficult conversations take place in one of three situations. The first is when you have to reveal something about yourself that you would rather other people not know. The second is when you have to deliver bad news. The third is when you have to resolve a conflict of interest with another person. Handling these conversations well requires practice.

The first of the three is the most straightforward. There is a simple rule here: any work-related piece of information about yourself that other people don't know and that you believe would reflect badly on you if they knew is something you should try to tell people as quickly as possible.

For example, if you make a mistake at work, you should own up to it immediately and then try to fix it. Successful work relationships are built on trust. You might think that you undermine that trust by admitting a mistake. But as I noted in chapter 5, managers are likely to trust you more if you own your mistakes right away than if you hide them. The sooner you admit a mistake and work to fix it, the less damage that mistake will cause. If you hide an error, you may compound its influence, because then nobody is working to repair it.

That doesn't mean it will be comfortable to admit mistakes. It will not. You may be embarrassed. In the moment, you may elicit a bad reaction from the person you tell. You may even get in trouble at work (though as I discuss in chapter 8, healthy organizations don't punish errors). However, in the long run, you're likely to learn more and to get more responsibility faster if you admit your mistakes and improve yourself than if you do not.

The second type of difficult conversation—delivering bad news—involves telling someone something they don't want to hear. As a result, despite your best efforts, they may not like you very much. Another one of the big five personality characteristics is agreeableness, which reflects your motivation to be liked by other people. The more agreeable you are, the harder it is to deliver bad news, and even if you aren't high in agreeableness, you probably don't relish doing so. You will dread even having the conversation. And when you finally get around to speaking, you may have trouble stating the news directly.

When you have to deliver bad news, do so in as constructive a way as possible. Sal is a supervisor with several direct reports. An employee who had worked for him for a year had not met expectations in her job. He had to tell her that he was putting her on probation. He started out by saying that he had to give some bad news. Then he went through the job criteria on which his employee had been unsatisfactory and said that he needed to put her on probation, describing exactly what that meant. Next he worked to frame this bad news as an opportunity. He reiterated that his company doesn't hire anyone it doesn't want to see succeed. He let her know what resources were available to help her improve her performance and told her that he was available to answer questions.

Sal clearly stated the bad news and what led to the negative evaluation. Critically, though, he made the conversation as productive as possible by highlighting the way forward rather than dwelling on the past.

The importance of being clear, empathetic, and productive is echoed in a story I was told by John Wright from the company Eagle's Flight. He said one of the most difficult lessons he had to learn as a leader was to provide clear and honest feedback to employees whose performance needed to improve. By being frank about both what was wrong and how to improve, he increased the number of opportunities he had to celebrate people's later accomplishments. The pain of difficult conversations was ultimately rewarded with the joy of sharing his people's success.

A related kind of bad news occurs when you have to deny a request. Marc Musick, a senior associate dean at the University of Texas, was addressing a group of emerging leaders. He talked about how he deals with situations in which he has to reject a request from a department. He said that he always treats these rejections as part of a problem-solving process: He lets the people making the request know that he cannot do exactly what they ask but presents alternatives that may help them achieve their goals. Then he offers to work with them to pursue those options.

Sometimes the bad news you have to deliver involves someone's having done something that violates a policy or requires correction. Lucienne had an employee who was causing disruption in her work group by getting angry and yelling whenever something went wrong. The first step she took toward having a productive discussion with him was to focus on his verifiable actions and talk about how people reacted to his outbursts.

It's tempting when discussing the actions of other people to slip into talk about their motives. That can make them defensive, because they may disagree with your characterization of the reasons behind their behavior. If you focus instead on what happened and how others reacted, you help avoid defensiveness. You can ask people to talk about why they acted as they did and then move to a discussion about how they might treat similar circumstances differently in the future.

Lucienne was able to get her employee to talk about his frustration with certain situations, and they worked out a plan for him to take a brief walk when he found himself unable to interact well with colleagues. During that walk, he would think about what he wanted to communicate about the situation and how to re-engage with his colleagues when he returned to their shared space.

The most difficult conversations occur when there's a conflict of interest between parties. That requires some negotiation or other method for resolving a dispute, because both parties cannot get what they want.

Conflicts of interest require the same skills we explored in chapter 4 when talking about negotiating job offers. When the conflict is serious, you must start by making sure you understand as much as possible about what the other person wants and why. Then, instead of fighting over whose request is more deserving of fulfillment, treat the conversation as a problem-solving exercise. Are there hidden resources that might allow one or both of you to get what you want in a different way? Is it possible to trade off in some way, such that one gets what they want right now and the other gets what they want the next time a conflict comes up?

This approach works particularly well when resolving conflicts with colleagues. There will inevitably be times when you and your colleagues want different things. Finding ways to work together for the good of the organization is crucial. In the long run, the most successful people are those who are most adept at creating novel solutions when resources are limited.

If your conflict with a colleague appears to be intractable, consider getting a neutral third party to mediate. Even when you adopt a problem-solving mindset for negotiations, the other party may have a hard time trusting you. In that case, it can be helpful for someone else to step in and work with the two of you to reach a resolution. Some companies even have an ombudsperson who mediates conflicts.

What It Means When You Think Communication Is Bad at Work

Employee engagement surveys have become a common way to assess the health of an organization. These surveys explore many aspects of the work environment, including salary, satisfaction with job duties, happiness with the management team, and effectiveness of organizational communications.

Often, one of the first big signs that an organization is having trouble is that employees give it low marks on communication. In response, organizations naturally try to improve how they communicate with employees. A common solution is to develop a newsletter or add mass emails to alert people about new initiatives. Although these changes are made with the best of intentions, they often fail to address the underlying problem, because the frequency or clarity of communications was not really what led to low marks on the survey.

Usually, what people really mean when they complain about communication is that in some instances they didn't have information they needed or wanted at a particular time. That may happen because the organization doesn't communicate frequently enough or clearly enough, but often it reflects other issues. The organization's decision-making process may not involve as many people as employees would like. People within the organization may disagree about the roles particular employees play, so one person doesn't know what information another person needs.

Several years ago, I worked with an academic group in which many employees complained that communication from management was poor. After extensive discussions, one of them pointed out that her job description was vague, so she was rarely certain which tasks she was supposed to take on and which to delegate to others. She expected her supervisor to be clearer about what jobs she was supposed to do. Her supervisor, meanwhile, believed that this employee understood which responsibilities were hers. So the fundamental problem was less about communication than about organizational structure and the clarity of people's roles.

Practically speaking, then, complaints about communication signal that people feel they aren't being informed of things they should know. Determining why they aren't getting that information requires additional work. It's important to start with specific cases in which someone failed to get needed information and then explore how information is normally transmitted in order to evaluate what actually needs to be done to fix the problem.

THE TAKEAWAYS

Your Brains

Motivational Brain

- Extraversion reflects how much you like to be at the center of attention in social situations.

- Narcissism reflects your belief that you are superior to others.

- Agreeableness reflects how much you want to be liked by other people.

Social Brain

- Communication is a coordinated activity among individuals; speakers and hearers actively participate in conversations.

- Often, we communicate indirectly in order to be polite.

- When conversing with a group in a shared space, we use many nonverbal cues to determine who should talk next. This is hard to do in virtual meetings.

Cognitive Brain

- Communication is best when small numbers of people are together in visual contact in real time. Deviations from this ideal increase opportunities for miscommunication.

- Mutual knowledge is the shared knowledge among speakers.

Your Tips

- Text communication requires skill at estimating what other people know.

- Text communication often wastes time, because turns in a conversation have gaps between them.

- Communicating too many requests via text can make you seem brusque.

- Phone calls permit access to tone of voice only; video conferences add facial expressions. It's hard to run group discussions or meetings using these modes.

- Be careful not to dominate meetings.

- Pay attention to the reactions other people have to your contributions in meetings.

- When running a meeting, engage in *backward design*.

- Learn to talk to others about the mistakes you make.

- Don't avoid hard conversations at work—develop strategies for having them.

- When you must say no to a request, find a way to be constructive.

- Complaints about communication at work are often actually about access to information.

7

Producing

You get a job or a promotion on the basis of your potential to benefit the organization you're working for. But your success in the job means realizing that potential. You actually need to get things done.

In a typical performance evaluation, some of your tasks or goals are laid out, and the evaluator determines whether you've met expectations in achieving them. The highest praise you can get is that you've exceeded expectations. You've gone beyond the potential your employers see in you and tried to make everyone around you more effective as well.

To exceed expectations, you need to take a big-picture view of what success means for you and make continual progress toward your goals. In this chapter, I start by exploring some of the overarching issues you should consider in defining success. Then I dig down to think about barriers you might face to being productive and ways to overcome them.

Beware of Systematic Failures

One of the most productive people I've ever met is Craig Wynett, who served for many years as the chief learning officer at Procter & Gamble. He reads voraciously, thinks deeply about ways to bring behavioral science to a large multinational corporation, and maintains a Rolodex of hundreds of experts he can call to get new insights into problems he's working on. In starting a conversation with him, it's common to ask, "How are you doing?" to which he invariably replies, "Pretty lazy."

I find this response memorable partly because I know that *lazy* is the last descriptor anyone would apply to Craig. More than that, though, it's a wonderful counterpoint to the typical response to this question, which is "Busy!" Almost everyone I know feels worked to the max. The day starts with a round of emails, followed by meetings, phone calls, reports, and more meetings. If you're like these "busy" people, when the workday ends, you have trouble figuring out what you got done. And you might not even leave work behind, because emails and texts will follow you for the rest of the night on your many connected devices.

A central problem with the epidemic of busyness is that you may do a lot of things without seeing them add up to something important. Peter Drucker made a wonderful distinction between *achievements* and *contributions* that is important to keep in mind. An achievement is something you can check off your to-do list during the day. Answering an email, attending a meeting, or finishing an analysis for a report is an achievement. A contribution is an important high-level goal that—when you look back over your work in the past—you're proud to have accomplished. Closing a significant business deal, writing a book, or launching a product is a contribution.

Your daily work life is (probably) filled with achievements. They constitute the variety of tasks that fill your time. But it takes some vigilance to ensure that they add up to a meaningful contribution.

Most organizations have a yearly evaluation process. Some of them are really good at getting people to think about what contributions they want to make over the coming year. It's important to take stock of your work each year, whether or not you're asked to do so. What do you really want to accomplish in the next year? What are the things you'll feel proud to have done?

At the same time, look back at the progress you've made over the previous year toward your hoped-for contributions. If you feel you accomplished something significant, you should celebrate that. But you should also look for the *systematic failures* in your past.

Probably some contribution you were hoping to make never materialized. You might have wanted to acquire a new skill, to bring a project to completion, or to change a policy at work. Flag any desired contributions you failed to make. That will tell you that if you keep doing the same things in the coming year, you'll continue to fail.

You have two reasonable reactions to systematic failures. One is to realize that a contribution you hoped to make is no longer truly a priority for you. In that case, you can remove it from your list of goals for the year to come. The other is to decide that the contribution really is important to you. Then you should look carefully at the tasks that occupy your daily routine. Unless you find ways to add more actions related to that contribution to your schedule, you'll continue to fail.

Tending Your Neighborhood

The sociologist Alan Fiske did a wonderful analysis of the main types of relationships people engage in. As you might expect, he gave them long and precise names. But three of the most important can be colloquially referred to as *family*, *neighbors*, and *strangers*. Your social brain is highly attuned to these.

Family includes the people you are closest to in life. You see them often and speak to them regularly. You participate in meals, rituals, and celebrations with them. Because these relationships are close, when you engage in transactions with family, you generally don't keep score. Parents take care of their children without ever sending them a bill for services rendered. Families find ways to support members who have fallen on hard times.

At the other end of the spectrum are strangers—people you don't know well or perhaps at all. You may engage in general conversation with them, but you don't have a trusted relationship. When you have a transaction with a stranger, it's fee-for-service. You pay for the goods you buy at a grocery store. If you get a flat tire on the highway and someone pulls over to assist you, you might thank them by offering money. Even if they refuse the gesture, it's an appropriate thing to do. You settle your debts with strangers in the moment, because you don't know whether you'll see them again or whether you can trust that they will follow through on their commitments.

In between are neighbors—people you know reasonably well. You talk to them frequently and include some personal details in the conversation. You may also have celebrations with them. This relationship creates a reasonable level of trust, so when you have a transaction with a neighbor, you can settle up over the long term. You can borrow a tool without paying a rental fee. If your neighbor helped you change a flat tire, you wouldn't offer cash as a way of saying thanks, but you might do a favor in return soon after. Neighbors pay attention to the balance of transactions. One who consistently fails to contribute will ultimately be kicked out of the neighborhood.

Ideally, organizations function like a neighborhood. You expect your colleagues to help you out when you need it, and you should do what you can to support them as well.* That leads to another dimension of productivity—not only do you complete your own tasks, but you help your colleagues make a contribution.

Become aware of key organizational priorities, and talk to your colleagues about what they want to accomplish. If you adopt organizational and collegial goals as your own, your motivational brain will help you notice when you might be able to do something that would facilitate them—even if you haven't been asked to do it.

When I was in college, I worked at a lumberyard. On weekdays, a big part of the job was loading up delivery trucks with supplies for contractors. Often, several orders were being filled early in the morning, and each of us would be assigned to get one of them ready to be loaded on a truck. One guy on the yard made a point of looking at all the lists so that if he was grabbing supplies that were needed for several orders, he could bring all of them to the staging area, eliminating much duplication of effort. His strategy soon became the norm among the crew.

Most of us will do something if a colleague asks. But to be proactive about maintaining your neighborhood, you have to consider other people's goals as well as your own. Then your motivational brain will naturally engage in what's called *opportunistic planning*. When you encounter an object or a person that's related to a goal you've adopted, your motivational brain will orient your cognitive brain to that object or person. When you bump into something that might assist your colleagues, you won't recognize the opportunity unless you've taken on their goals.

---

*A few organizations strive to establish other relationships among employees. Notably, the military needs soldiers to have a family relationship. Soldiers are expected to be willing to die for one another, which is a debt that cannot be repaid. Thus many of the rituals in military training are designed to create a family from people who started as strangers. Similarly, nonprofits may treat their donors like family, because big donors make contributions that can never be repaid in kind.

Being a good neighbor brings you recognition for your positive contributions and your leadership potential. Of course, helping your colleagues doesn't mean prioritizing them over yourself—you still need to make your own contribution to the workplace. Simply alerting a colleague to an opportunity is still a collegial thing to do.

Barriers to Productivity

Just knowing what contribution you want to make doesn't guarantee you'll be able to make it (sadly). Many factors can keep you from reaching your goals. Many of the barriers to productivity reside in your own actions at work. Some of them relate to the actions of colleagues. And institutional factors may keep you from making your contribution.

Individual Factors

One important reason to get to know yourself is so that you can do a good job of managing yourself and your workload to be most effective. Let's start with your body and brain.

BODY AND BRAIN

Many people think of the brain as being like a computer. Your computer doesn't care how much it has been used recently. Turn it on, and it's ready to go. You may be prone to treat your brain as if it were independent of your body. Sure, you may be tired, but a little caffeine will perk you up and get you through the day. But the state of your body has a profound impact on the state of your mind.

Perhaps the most important thing you can do for your productivity is get regular sleep. People differ a lot in how much sleep they need, and the amount you need will probably change over the course of your life. You can do a pretty simple test to learn whether you're getting enough sleep. Read something complex during an afternoon when you haven't had any caffeine in the previous few hours. If you have trouble focusing and find yourself dozing off, you're not getting enough sleep.

Good sleep affects all aspects of your brain. Your motivational brain will stay more focused on the goals you're trying to achieve. Your emotional state will be better. Sleep partly resets a brain structure called the amygdala, which is associated with responses to fear and anxiety. And it helps you separate your emotional response to a situation from the memory of that situation, so negative memories are less likely to depress your mood if you sleep regularly.

The younger you are, the more you may be affected immediately by sleep disruption. In your twenties, a bad night's sleep can make it hard to concentrate the next day and difficult to learn new material. As you get older, the negative effects of sleep deprivation are more long-term than short-term. Poor sleep in middle age won't necessarily make the next day bad, but consistently getting poor sleep in middle age is associated with cognitive problems in old age.

Most people deal with sleep deprivation chemically rather than by getting more sleep. Chances are, you drink some caffeine every day. Caffeine makes you feel alert, even on days when you haven't gotten enough sleep. However, studies suggest that sleep enhances your cognitive brain by helping you remember things you're learning, while caffeine does not. But not all is lost. A nap is much more effective than caffeine in helping you learn, and it will restore other brain functions as well.

Aerobic exercise, too, improves productivity. A variety of studies in children, young adults, and older adults suggest that regular exercise (at least thirty minutes a day) improves aspects of the cognitive brain such as attention and memory and also overall brain health. Exercise is particularly important for ensuring that your brain remains healthy in your later years, keeping you productive throughout your life.

IDEAL ENGAGEMENT

Typically, you want to get as much done as you can every day, yet your list of tasks to be accomplished can feel never-ending. The first thing you should do is get a grip on what you actually need to accomplish. That means keeping an agenda or a to-do list so that important tasks don't fall through the cracks. Next, set aside the time to actually do them.

Don't rely on your cognitive brain to keep track of the tasks you need to do. Humans developed writing for a reason. Human memory is great for pulling up information relevant to your immediate situation. When you see a colleague, you may be reminded of previous conversations with that colleague, or of something you promised to do. But your memory is less good for keeping track of arbitrary lists of things, such as your agenda. That's particularly true when a list requires frequent revision. In addition, you don't get much time to study the items on your schedule, so you're better off writing them all down in one place.

Here are a few strategies for making your to-do list. First, estimate how much time each task will take. Then, if you find yourself with a spare fifteen minutes, you can knock off a short task instead of getting sucked into the black hole of your email queue. Second, look over your list each day and reprioritize it. Some items may be at the bottom because their deadlines were far away when you first wrote them down—but deadlines have a way of creeping up on you.

You should have a calendar as well as a to-do list. Early in your career, you may think you don't need one, because you don't have a lot of meetings on your schedule. But the number of claims on your calendar will slowly grow, so you may not realize how much of your time is spoken for before you've even had a chance to get started on your to-do list.

A key reason for maintaining a calendar is so that you can block out time to work on list items that relate to your long-term goals. You can also put items with long deadlines on your calendar, choosing a date when you can comfortably work on a given task to complete it on time.

How much time is a reasonable amount to complete a task? To answer that question, I'll invoke the Yerkes-Dodson curve—a concept that Robert Yerkes and John Dodson introduced in 1908. Psychologists studying the motivational brain have long known that you won't make progress toward your goals unless those goals are active—or, in the parlance of psychology, *aroused*. When a goal has a low level of arousal, you don't do much to achieve it. As the arousal level goes up, so does your performance—up to a point. Yerkes and Dodson proposed that increases in arousal eventually lead to a decrease in performance. Think of this overarousal as panic—you have so much energy that you aren't functioning effectively. So there's an optimal level of arousal for outstanding performance.

People differ in their resting level of arousal. Look around at those you know. Some people are constantly motivated to get things done. They like to finish tasks well ahead of schedule. Others have a lower resting level. They need to be kick-started before they accomplish something on a project, and a close deadline is what really motivates them. Casey told me that she learned in college that she's more productive when she has a lot to do rather than just a few projects. That's a sign of low arousal. People like Casey need a certain amount of chaos to feel that they're firing on all cylinders. That much work would drive a high-arousal person over the edge of the Yerkes-Dodson curve.

So again, you have to get to know yourself as well as the people around you. How much energy do you need to be ready to work? How much arousal is too much for you? The aim is to manage your workload so that you stay in that sweet spot where you have enough energy to be motivated but not so much that you can no longer make progress.

Sometimes you may have to work with someone whose resting level of arousal is different from yours. If you're a high-arousal person and your colleague is a low-arousal one, you may have problems—you may need something from the other person that they don't get to until the deadline is so close that your sweet spot has passed. When you recognize this possibility, coordinate with your colleague to ensure that you get what you need to work optimally. And if you're a low-arousal person, you may want to set false deadlines for yourself to ensure that you help your high-arousal colleagues work effectively.

Another factor affecting your arousal is the number of technological alerts you get. Email, text messages, instant messages, and phones will try to interrupt you throughout the day. Paige, who mentors people at her workplace, coaches everyone to turn off as many alerts as they can. All these alarms increase arousal levels and distract you from your tasks, undermining productivity.

Alerts are also an invitation to multitask. Decades of psychology research on the cognitive brain, typically done under the heading of *dual task performance* (a fancy way of saying "doing two things at once"), demonstrates that when you interleave two tasks, you become worse at both of them. When the executive-functioning part of your cognitive brain has to shift back and forth between tasks, performance declines.

This task switching creates two problems. One, information related to the first task you are doing has to be dampened, and information related to the second task has to be activated. That takes time. Two, when you return to the first task, you've probably lost your place, which leads to a further slowdown in your work. So you'll be most productive when you focus first on one task and then on another. Removing alerts from your environment is a great way to keep from multitasking.

To manage your tasks, you also need to decide what you should take on and what you should refuse. Andy told me that he sees many new employees accept too much work, assuming it's a good career move, only to see the overload kill their productivity. The number of hours you can work in a week truly is limited, so focus your efforts as much as possible on items that will help you make your contribution. When you're asked to take on something new, consider the other entries on your to-do list to ensure that you don't crowd out valuable tasks.

A recurring theme in this book is that saying no can be hard, even though it's important to stand up for yourself. I've already mentioned that agreeableness is a core personality characteristic. If you're an agreeable person, you don't want to turn down other people's requests. A related issue affects people high in conscientiousness. As discussed in chapter 5, conscientious people like to complete tasks, so they're motivated to help get things done around the organization. Both these characteristics can lead people to take on more than they can handle and then to feel bad when they don't succeed.

Luckily, two strategies are available to people who have difficulty saying no. You can begin by asking permission to turn down a request. You can say you're really swamped at the moment and ask whether someone else might be able to handle it. That way, you'll learn which requests you can safely pass along to someone else. And if the request is something you really do need to take on, you can ask for help delegating something on your to-do list to someone else. Look at high-priority or time-consuming list items and ask for recommendations for who might be able to take them on so that you can focus on the new request. It's better to maintain a manageable list of tasks than to disappoint people by failing to complete things you promised to do.

THE VALUE OF TIME AWAY FROM WORK

The saying "All work and no play makes Jack a dull boy" dates back to the seventeenth century. Whoever coined this phrase was on to something. Stepping away from your work regularly makes good sense.

As I mentioned earlier in this chapter, sleep and exercise are important for brain health, and it's hard to get either of them while you're at work. Chances are, you've encountered discussions about

JAZZ BRAIN:

The Perfect Is the Enemy of the Good

If you listen to a lot of jazz, you've no doubt heard some great solos. In the face of these amazing performances, you could be forgiven for being reluctant to blow a solo of your own. After all, you're likely to make some mistakes. At a minimum, you may not measure up to the standards set by the greats who came before you.

Kristen, a veterinarian, said that the biggest productivity killer in her field is perfectionism—it keeps people from being decisive and from delegating tasks to others who might not carry them out as well as they themselves would.

To be successful, though, you have to be willing to try things that you haven't yet perfected. In general, the best project is a completed project—even if it has flaws. Any large project has facets that could be improved. Those improvements can be made later. Remember that even the best performers in your field started somewhere. You may not see their early mistakes, but that doesn't mean they never made—and don't continue to make—them.

Finally, you must be willing to delegate. As you advance in your career, you'll gain expertise that allows you to do things that other people cannot. Focus your efforts on those things. Pass along tasks that others can do well enough, even if you think you could do them better.

"work-life balance." Not all the big-picture goals you want to achieve in your life have to do with work. Personal, romantic, and family relationships require time away from work. Hobbies add richness to your life. And Earth has many beautiful places to visit.

Of course, work-life balance doesn't mean that every day, week, or month must be perfectly balanced. Sometimes you have to emphasize particular facets of your life at the expense of others. As a graduate student and a young professor, I tilted the balance toward work in order to complete my education, begin my career, and get tenure. After I had children, that balance shifted more toward family. The key is to evaluate on a yearly basis how you feel about the amount of time you spend on work and on other pursuits to see whether you're happy with the choices you've made. The end of the calendar year (when people often contemplate New Year's resolutions) is a good time to think broadly about your priorities.

Even when your focus is primarily on work, you have good reasons to step away from what you're doing. For one thing, the other experiences you have in life can feed back into your work life in unexpected ways. I would not have "Jazz Brain" sections in this book were it not for the time I spend each week listening to music, practicing the saxophone, and playing with my band.

Time away from work enhances your cognitive brain and makes you a better problem solver. For one thing, your memory tends to get stuck on particular solutions. The information you retrieve from memory inhibits alternatives that might also help you solve a problem. When you walk away from a problem, your memory resets, allowing you to go back and get different information.

I've mentioned some benefits of regular sleep. Another one is that you tend to lose some of the details of things you're working on, so your description of a problem becomes more abstract. "Sleeping on" a difficult problem allows this more abstract description to pull information from your memory that differs from what you retrieved the previous day.

For all these reasons, it's a good idea to get away from your work frequently.

Social Factors

You aren't in complete control of your own productivity. Colleagues and supervisors can have a profound influence on what you do. You must overcome challenges to working effectively with the people around you. And the modern organizational environment can present barriers, such as an open office environment or the need to work remotely. I touch on these issues in this section.

BAD NEIGHBORS

Earlier in this chapter, I suggested that you should find ways to support your neighborhood. Unfortunately, not everyone you work with interacts in the same way. Some organizations reward individual achievement over teamwork, and some people look out primarily for themselves. You need to ask whether this environment is one in which you can thrive.

A growing amount of work on personality has focused on what is called the *dark triad*: psychopathy, Machiavellianism, and narcissism. *Psychopaths* are emotionally cold and tend to be manipulative, impulsive, charming, and deceitful. *Machiavellianism* is a tendency to manipulate other people toward one's own ends. *Narcissists* believe that they're better than everyone else and should be listened to. Many narcissists use accolades to bolster their self-esteem, so they can become angry when their authority is challenged.

Colleagues who display these tendencies create a bad work environment. They may try to manipulate you for their own benefit without regard to the impact on your career. They may seek to take the credit for a team's successes and to deflect blame onto others for failures.

If you detect these characteristics in colleagues, do what you can to insulate yourself from the most negative consequences of their behavior. Talk to a supervisor about your concerns. Document your interactions with these individuals in case they ever try to blame you for a problem.

The most difficult situation to deal with is when your boss displays the characteristics of the dark triad. A narcissistic boss will soak up credit for the group's success rather than enhancing your career. Working for someone like this provides little long-term benefit.

Try to find allies in other groups and look to transfer to another unit. In the short term, you can make your best ideas seem like the boss's ideas so that you can pursue projects you want to work on. But don't expect credit if those ventures succeed.

EFFECTIVE TEAMWORK

Even when everyone wants to collaborate well, it's not always easy to work as a team. Most of your education focused on individual excellence. You probably didn't get much explicit training in how to mesh your talents with those of other people or how to construct an effective team. Studies suggest that just choosing the best individual performers may not lead to the best group outcomes. Research by John Hildreth and Cameron Anderson found that when a group consists entirely of people in leadership roles, its problem-solving performance is worse than when it includes both people who typically lead and people who typically follow. Whole books have been written on teamwork, of course, but I want to hit a few key points related to productivity.

Just as a basketball team needs players with varying skills on the court, your work team needs to meld a set of skills. Here's a good initial list of desirable members.

- Someone with an overall vision of what the team is trying to accomplish.

- Someone who is highly conscientious and will ensure that team members have specific tasks to do and complete them in a timely fashion.

- Someone with domain expertise in the problems you're trying to solve.

- Someone who can communicate effectively about the work being done.

- For innovation projects, an expert generalist (as discussed in chapter 5).

- At least two people who exhibit moderate to low agreeableness and are thus willing to criticize and raise objections.

Of course, some people may meet several of these criteria, so your group needn't be enormous.

With groups, you need to manage the thinking and doing of your motivational brain (which I introduced in chapter 4). Group dynamics can influence motivation to complete a task. Often, groups latch on to the first solution to a problem, wanting to adopt it and move along. To ensure that your group has enough time to deliberate, set a particular time or date for reaching a final decision. That will reduce people's tendency to want to finish quickly. Make sure you give everyone on the team plenty of time to contribute so that you don't miss out on key perspectives. And don't just go along with what everyone else says—contribute to the conversation yourself. You want the group to remain in a thinking mode while generating possible solutions to a problem and to transition to a doing mode when you're ready to implement a particular course of action.

The last key element of effective teams is willingness to do a follow-up analysis of the team's performance. Such follow-ups are sometimes called debriefings or (in military terminology) after-action reports. Scott Tannenbaum and Christopher Cerasoli did a nice review of the value of debriefings. Several qualities characterize those that improve team performance.

- Participants are actively willing to learn what went right and what went wrong.

- The debriefing is framed as an opportunity to learn rather than an attempt to evaluate group performance.

- It focuses on specific events, not generalities.

- It involves input from a variety of team members, not just leaders or independent observers.

Debriefings like this help team members learn how to collaborate more effectively and determine whether the team has gaps that need to be addressed for future work.

MANAGING YOUR ENVIRONMENT

Your work environment is another significant factor in your productivity. Fifty years ago, the environment was fairly homogeneous. People occupied an office alone or with a small number of colleagues. They arrived in the morning and left at the end of the workday (with occasional overtime). They may have done some amount of work-related travel or visited clients or customers.

Now a number of work environments exist, and you may experience many of them over time. Although some people still work in traditional offices, open-office plans with cubicles (full height or half height) are popular. In "hot-desking" offices, people have no assigned work space; they choose one each day they're on the premises. Some people work remotely, either every day or a few days a week.

These environments are intended to give people more flexibility in how they engage with work. They take advantage of advances in information technology that allow connection to the workplace even from a distance. They also aim to promote collaboration by not sequestering people in offices.

However, these environments present challenges. It can be hard to develop consistent work habits if your environment changes daily. Open-office environments are distracting. Your visual system is attuned to motion, so someone standing up and looking around in a cubicle environment (sometimes called *prairie-dogging*) can be very distracting, as can the many conversations going on in a cubicle environment. Research by Lauren Emberson, Gary Lupyan, Michael Goldstein, and Michael Spivey suggests that listening to half a conversation (which happens when you hear someone talking on the phone) is particularly distracting, because your auditory system can't predict the way the conversation will progress. Studies also suggest that you're much worse at learning new information when you hear conversations going on around you than when you're working someplace quiet.

To be more productive in your environment, do what you can to support your work habits. Habits require consistency. Take a few moments to set up your work space so that everything is where you expect it to be, whether you're working from home, remotely, or at a shared desk. That way, you won't constantly be searching for basic supplies or other objects you need. Try to do your work in the same location as often as possible to create a work mindset.

If you're working from home, create spaces that allow you to get away from work. Constant internet connectivity and smartphones make it hard enough to separate from your work, and if your workplace is also your home, you'll get constant reminders of work you haven't finished yet. At a minimum, have one space in your home where you never work and use that space as a sanctuary when you're feeling stressed about your job. I have a music room at home where I play my saxophone. I never do any work there, so it's a protected space.

If you're working in an open office or in a public place, such as a coffee shop or a coworking space, find ways to minimize distraction. Research suggests that music or white noise helps some people but not others stay focused. Some studies show, for example, that introverts are more distracted than extroverts by background noise. So if you're in a shared environment and find the atmosphere distracting, experiment with different kinds of background noise (but recognize that they may not work for you). Alternatively, if you have a task that requires focus, find a quiet location to work on it. Many open-office environments have private rooms you can use when you need a break from the hubbub.

Finally, work with your colleagues to manage your availability for quick conversations. When you're interrupted for even a short conversation, you may need several minutes to get back on task, and that can deal a blow to your productivity. Try to develop a system that alerts your colleagues when interruptions are fine and when you'd prefer to work without distraction. Many cubicle farms have begun to use red, yellow, and green pointers to signal openness to interruption; red means "Do not disturb," yellow means "I would prefer not to be disturbed," and green means you're available for conversation.

If you're having a hard time getting work done, play around with your environment to learn what will allow you to be the most productive. Once you have a good sense of how you work best, chat with your supervisor to see if you can structure your setup to accomplish your goals while still being available to your colleagues when needed.

Institutional Factors

In the short term, stress can focus you on your work. When something goes wrong, for example, you may be able to accomplish a lot in a short time to fix the problem. Chronic stress, though, is a productivity killer. Stress is the reaction of your motivational brain to situations in which you're trying to avoid some negative outcome. Unfortunately, the workplace itself can sometimes be the source of stress.

In chapter 2, I talked about the importance of understanding your own values for the work you do. As you get to know the organization you work for, you may find that its values diverge from yours in some way, which can make it hard for you to get work done. In chapter 9, I discuss ways to think about these value conflicts as you consider future jobs.

Other institutional factors that influence productivity relate to how leaders affect what people do. In chapter 8, I examine the alignment between what an organization wants, what people are visibly doing, and what the organization rewards. In this section, though, I want to talk about bias in the workplace that may affect productivity. In the fall of 2017, the *New York Times* detailed allegations of sexual harassment against the film producer Harvey Weinstein, which led to a public discussion of harassment. Harassment at work on the basis of sex, race, ethnicity, religion, or sexual orientation is not new, but that scandal has made organizations more willing to confront it rather than sweep it under the rug.

If you feel you've been discriminated against or harassed on the basis of some characteristic of who you are, that is an organizational problem that must be addressed. It creates tremendous chronic stress to face mistreatment at work. You need to sit down with a supervisor as soon as possible to talk about what happened. Large organizations may have particular people (often in HR) who can take your complaint and initiate a process to deal with it. Even if you're relatively new to an organization, you shouldn't sit idly by if you're the victim of bias or harassment.

It is the responsibility of everyone in an organization to set the tone for what's acceptable. If you see something happen to someone else in the workplace that makes you uncomfortable, say something to a supervisor. If you're in a leadership position, sit down with people who have done something wrong and talk to them about it—sooner rather than later. Organizations benefit from diversity, but the benefit is achieved only if the workplace accepts the diversity.

You may learn things about yourself. If someone speaks to you about a comment you made or an action you took, take responsibility. You may not have intended to create any discomfort in your colleagues, but often you're not the best judge of how your comments and actions are interpreted by others. You can apologize for the impact you've had and learn how to create a more harmonious workplace for everyone.

The issue of harassment in the workplace is controversial, because shifting social norms can change what's considered acceptable behavior in the workplace. For instance, if you watch movies or TV shows about the 1960s, you see a lot of smoking. In the modern workplace, most office buildings are smoke-free, but many people resisted that transition as it occurred. Similarly, some people continue to decry the embrace of diversity as mere "political correctness."

The many high-profile cases of harassment in the workplace demonstrate that organizations have a hard time policing themselves. The fundamental problem here resides in the motivational brain, which is wired to do what feels best in the short term rather than what is right in the long term. An accusation—or even evidence—that someone in your organization has harassed someone else sets up a confrontation. Leadership has to investigate the complaint and act against people who have been credibly accused. Negative publicity for the organization may result.

In the short term, it often seems easier to do nothing at all. Perhaps this was an isolated incident. Perhaps the complaint will go away. Kicking the can down the road may save a short-term hassle, but it creates several long-term problems. First, it sends a message to harassers that their actions have no consequences, which can put other people at risk. Second, it often increases negative publicity in the long run if an organization is shown to have a history of ignoring complaints. Third, it creates an atmosphere in the workplace in which people are constantly on guard.

To make leaders willing to investigate claims in a timely fashion, we must change the way we train people to deal with harassment. Most compliance training systems treat the problem abstractly. People are given definitions of unacceptable behaviors and perhaps a few examples. Everyone agrees to be on the lookout for violations and to report them. But the training doesn't expose people to the tension between the short-term desire to ignore a complaint and the long-term need to address it. Nor does it give them a sense of what their involvement will be if they do report something they experience or witness.

Organizations need to teach their people how to take action that will benefit the organization in the long run rather than doing what feels expedient in the short run.

Diversity and Inclusion

A good business case can be made for the value of diversity. Workplaces that include a variety of perspectives are creative, find ways to solve new problems, and can capitalize on trends. To be clear, people must be able to bring their authentic selves to work. That doesn't mean they need to feel comfortable in their work at all times, but their discomfort shouldn't stem from who they are.

Diversity is not sufficient, though. Its cousin *inclusion* is also necessary. Inclusion involves going beyond merely hiring a wide variety of people. Everyone should have an opportunity to contribute to the work being done in a way that acknowledges the differences in perspective and life experience that people bring to the workplace.

In many ways, diversity is easier for organizations to develop than inclusion. Organizations must strive to hire a diverse workforce, but they can easily survey the demographic characteristics of employees to ensure that a range of people have been hired. It's harder to ensure that everyone plays a role at work and that what may make people different from others is accepted socially. Leaders should set an example that encourages participation.

THE TAKEAWAYS

Your Brains

Motivational Brain

- Achievements are tasks you tick off your to-do list, whereas contributions are significant goals you look back on with pride.
- Systematic failures signal that you need to change a behavior to achieve a particular goal.
- The Yerkes-Dodson curve suggests that there's an optimal level of arousal for task performance.
- The dark triad of negative personality characteristics encompasses psychopathy, Machiavellianism, and narcissism.
- The motivational system prefers actions whose benefit is in the short term to those whose benefit is in the long term.

Social Brain

- Most relationships in your life can be characterized as being with family, neighbors, or strangers.

Cognitive Brain

- Active goals affect what you see in the environment, enabling opportunistic planning.
- Regular sleep enhances learning and reduces anxiety.
- The human mind doesn't multitask; it toggles between tasks.

Your Tips

- Each year, note your systematic failures.
- To be a good neighbor, adopt some of your colleagues' goals.
- Get regular sleep, exercise, and eat well.

- Keep a good to-do list and an agenda.
- Find the sweet spot in your arousal level so that you can get work done without panic.
- Focus on one task at a time as often as possible.
- Learn to say no to requests to avoid becoming overcommitted.
- Be sure to take breaks from work.
- Work when you're at work, and don't work when you're not.
- Find ways to avoid colleagues who have dark triad characteristics.
- Learn the composition of a good team.
- Use debriefings to improve team performance.
- Harassment cannot be tolerated in the workplace. Although it may be tempting to avoid addressing it, the long-term ramifications for an organization will be bad.
- Diversity in organizations has value, but only if the diverse individuals are included in the work being done.

8

Leading

Human beings may be a cooperative species, but to get everyone working together toward a common goal, organizations have to know where they want to go and how to get there. That is the job of leadership.

I had the opportunity to work on a leadership education plan for the University of Texas. Our goal was not to train every one of our students to be a leader, though we certainly hope that many of them will take leadership roles in their careers. Instead, we wanted students to understand what good leadership is so that they can practice it and can recognize when they are working with an effective leader.

A lot of ink has been spilled trying to distinguish between *leadership* and its cousin *management*. People use the words in varying ways, which makes providing a strict definition difficult. But it's clear that people in leadership roles need to engage in both *strategic* and *operational* tasks. The strategic component involves determining the vision and direction of an organization, making decisions about how to pursue that vision, and motivating people to join in. The operational component implements that vision by allocating resources, evaluating progress toward the goal, and correcting the plan when a goal isn't being reached.

From this perspective, if your job involves a higher ratio of strategic to operational tasks, you're in a leadership role, whereas if the reverse is true, you're in a management role. That said, both roles require at least some strategic and some operational work.

Research by Jasmine Vergauwe and colleagues suggests that charismatic leaders—who have a high degree of self-confidence, communicate well with others, and are open to creative problem solving—are excellent at the strategic component of leadership but often overestimate the importance of strategy over operations in running an organization. The most successful leaders can motivate people to engage in a shared vision and also put specific plans and procedures in place that will allow the organization to realize that vision. No single person needs to be highly skilled both strategically and operationally, but everyone should recognize the importance of these components.

We often confuse leadership with leadership roles. That is, we assume that to be a leader, someone must occupy a particular position of authority in the organizational hierarchy. If you are someone's supervisor, for example, you have the authority to evaluate their performance and (perhaps) their pay. But leading other people involves more than having the authority to make a request or give an order. After all, since you were a child you've known that "Because I said so" is a poor reason to do what someone asks.

Leaders find ways to create shared goals among a group. That means that even people low on the organizational chart can lead. No matter what authority you have, you can influence someone else's actions by your example, your encouragement, your expertise, and your feedback. That's why everyone in an organization knows who the real leaders are, regardless of the titles they hold.

When we set out to define how to teach leadership at the University of Texas, we focused on certain skills that people can develop and recognize in others, including:

- Being able to delegate tasks

- Thinking critically and possessing decision-making skills

- Taking personal responsibility for actions

- Communicating effectively and speaking in public

- Fostering collaboration

- Engaging in ethical leadership

I organize this chapter around those elements.

Delegating

A core leadership skill is delegating work. When you delegate a task to someone, you have to trust that the person knows what has to be done, will do it well, and will ask for help if necessary. Leaders can do several things to achieve this level of trust: Endeavor to develop other people's talents. Treat errors appropriately. Ensure that you align rewards in the organization with desired outcomes.

Developing Others

A significant component of leadership is helping the people around you improve and grow into their roles. Just as you shouldn't expect to have mastered every aspect of a new job when you take it, you shouldn't expect the people working for and with you to know how to do everything the first time they're asked to do it. Helping them hone their skills is crucial.

That may be harder than it sounds, because the first time you ask someone to do an unfamiliar task, having them do it and then giving them feedback will take longer than doing it yourself would. But you won't be able to turn over tasks to people until you're sure they can do a reasonable job on their own, so you have to sacrifice time now in order to save it later.

Time spent training the people around you is not wasted. It's common to think about productivity primarily in terms of what you accomplish yourself. But as you progress in your career—particularly when you take on leadership roles—you're also judged by whether the people working for you are productive.

Errors as Learning Experiences

The path to creating a culture in which people want to develop emerges from how you treat mistakes. I discussed the importance of mistakes in chapter 5 when talking about learning. Now I explore how you treat mistakes from a leadership standpoint. You may think that the more costly a potential mistake, the more the threat of punishment should surround it, so that people will be vigilant for errors. This approach is 180 degrees wrong, however.

Consider aviation. Mistakes in air travel can have devastating consequences. But aviation catastrophes are not generally caused by a single error. Rather, they result from a cascade of errors. Consequently, the US Federal Aviation Administration has implemented the Aviation Safety Action Program (ASAP), whereby members of the industry who report errors they make within twenty-four hours won't be punished for their mistakes—provided they did nothing illegal, such as drinking alcohol on the job. The program is administered by a separate agency (NASA) to create confidence that error reporting won't have negative career consequences.

This program recognizes that people don't make mistakes because they lack incentives to avoid them. They make them because humans are fallible. The way to ensure air-traffic safety is not to design procedures that will eliminate any possibility of error; it is to design them so that the errors people make don't have devastating results. That can be done only by cataloguing all the errors made and studying them to find patterns. Aviation is safe because it embraces mistakes and learns from them.

After all, if you punish mistakes, people's primary incentive will be to hide them. People don't go out of their way to invite punishment. But a hidden problem cannot be fixed; and if it stays hidden long enough, it may turn into a catastrophe. Aim to punish negligence rather than mistakes. If someone working normally makes a mistake, treat it as a learning opportunity—even if it has significant consequences. Only someone who doesn't prepare, doesn't try, and doesn't attempt to learn from prior mistakes should be punished.

Reward Structures

Asking people to do something is only part of what informs the actions they take. A core principle that reflects the operation of the motivational brain is: there is what you say, what you do, and what you reward, and people listen to those elements in reverse order. What you say (or what you request) has the smallest influence on their daily behavior. People who work for you are also watching what you and others in the organization are doing and modeling their behavior accordingly. Most important, they are observing the behavior that gets rewarded. Rewards come in a variety of forms, including promotions, opportunities, access to resources, and attention.

When you're a leader, it can be frustrating to ask consistently for a particular behavior and not get it. If that happens, it's highly likely that what you say you want doesn't align with what people are obviously doing and being rewarded for. You need to be vigilant for such misalignment.

A common example involves innovation. Companies talk frequently about how important it is for them to innovate. Indeed, at many companies where I have spoken, the mission statement is proudly displayed near the entrance, and more often than not it says something about the importance of innovation. Yet few companies are truly innovative.

Part of the problem is that very little of the work people are doing is focused on finding new approaches to products and processes. Instead, most activities are in support of the status quo (and incremental improvements). You're not likely to start taking time out of your day to work on an innovative project if you don't see anyone else engaged in that sort of work.

Furthermore, many companies, particularly large organizations, have reward structures that are biased against innovation. Managers may be given bonuses based on the quarterly or yearly profitability of their units, while innovation is expensive in the short term and typically doesn't produce benefits for a while. And innovations that fail (which many do) will never produce a payoff. In a bonus environment like this, managers have little incentive to support innovative projects. Furthermore, the people who are getting promoted in an organization are often those who are making steady progress. Innovative projects don't display consistent growth. For a long time, they generate no revenues, and then suddenly (if they succeed) they take off. Organizations that want more innovation must reset their reward structures to promote innovative projects.

Pay attention to all these factors driving behavior. Look at how they influence people to do things that aren't what you asked for. A key observation about the social brain is that when we evaluate the behavior of other people, we focus on their traits and deemphasize their goals and the situational factors that might also be driving them.

This happens even though we often pay a lot of attention to the situation and to our goals when explaining our own behavior.

Practically speaking, when colleagues don't do what they're supposed to, you're probably inclined to wonder what's wrong with them. You may assume they have traits that prevent them from performing as expected. Perhaps they're incompetent or unmotivated. Before ascribing their behavior to some personal aspect, examine the work situation to determine its influence on behavior. It may be that any competent person in that situation would act in the same way.

Critical Thinking, Problem Solving, and Decision Making

The strategic and operational parts of leadership both require clear decisions that are made with as much knowledge as possible. A great deal has been written about decision biases that can lead people to make poor choices. In this section, I want to focus on a few elements of decision making that are important in leadership contexts.

Learning to Say Yes and No

Think about the requests people make of you. How do you generally respond? If you're like most of us, you have a dominant response. Some people are prone to assent to requests. Greg told me about an old boss who thought every idea was a great one. He truly wanted to see people achieve their goals, so he would say yes to almost everything. As a result, his resources were stretched so thin that few of the projects he agreed to support actually succeeded. In contrast, some people tend to turn down almost everything. I was once chatting with a colleague from another university who jokingly referred to his dean (who controlled the resources for his college) as Dr. No, because the dean almost never agreed to move any projects forward. Eventually, people just stopped going to the dean with new ideas.

As a leader, you need to be comfortable saying both yes and no. In the section on difficult conversations in chapter 6, I discussed how an agreeable person finds it hard to give someone bad news. If you're agreeable, you have to practice turning people down when they ask for something. Two ways of saying no are important here. One is that if you'd really like to support a project but can't do it right away or as it has been presented, suggest a few alternatives you might be able to support. Encourage continued discussion even when you can't grant a specific request.

The other is for when someone approaches you with a project that you think is simply a nonstarter. Agreeable people are tempted to be encouraging by saying something such as "I'd like to help, but . . ." and then blaming some circumstance for their inability to support the request. The problem with this approach is that whoever made the request will probably keep working on the project in the hope of finding some way to address the reason you gave for saying no. If you think a project shouldn't move forward, take responsibility for that decision. Say you're deciding not to pursue the project. Give super-visees constructive feedback to help them understand what kinds of requests you might support in the future. But don't say things that give people false hope.

When saying no, it's important to be clear about why, because you might be turning down something you should consider more seriously. As I mentioned in chapter 2, the personality characteristic openness to experience reflects the orientation that people take to new things and new ideas. People high in openness will embrace a new idea, even if they ultimately decide it's not something they want to pursue, while those low in openness will reject new ideas just because they're new. Leaders who are low in openness may miss out on valuable opportuni-ties. That is, they have trouble saying "yes."

Pat worked for a company that invented but didn't pursue a number of technologies that are now common in people's daily experience with computers. He told me about a messaging system the company had developed in the early days of the internet which allowed employees to set up interest groups to discuss topics. Most of the interest groups focused on work problems, though some inevitably focused on entertainment and hobbies. Employees loved the groups, which were useful for allowing people around the world to weigh in on problems being worked on. But the company shut down the system out of concern that people were wasting too much time on things unrelated to work. It didn't do a real cost-benefit analysis, nor did it attempt to find ways to adapt the system to the work flow. Instead, it pulled the plug on a technology that could have significantly boosted productivity decades before nearly everyone on planet Earth was using social networks.

When you hear a new idea and you have a negative reaction, think carefully about why you have concerns. In the absence of a reason for your reaction, you may be rejecting it primarily because it's new. And even if you have a reason, it may not be a good one. Many companies, for example, have neglected to pursue innovative projects because they were afraid to disrupt their current business. They are failing to consider that if a new technology is going to disrupt their business, they should be the ones to bring it to market.

Kodak, the leading producer of photographic film, is a classic example. Kodak originally developed digital imaging technology but chose not to bring it to market for fear that it would cannibalize the film business. The company was correct that digital imaging would disrupt the photography industry, but because of its strategic decision, it failed to benefit from the disruption.

Not every firm is afraid of industry-disrupting changes. For example, in the late 1990s, Netflix came to prominence with a business that enabled people to rent movies on DVD via the postal service. This model was so successful that Netflix contributed to the downfall of the giant brick-and-mortar movie rental company Blockbuster. But when high-speed internet became common in people's homes, Netflix shifted from DVD rentals to streaming movies over the internet. It could easily have elected not to shift to streaming because that would undermine its core business. But given the limitations of the postal service for transferring computer files, it recognized that its original business model would not be successful in the long term.

A willingness to disrupt the core business is related to what economists call *sunk costs*. A sunk cost is any resource (such as time, money, or effort) that has already been spent on a particular project. Economists argue that you shouldn't consider sunk costs when you're making decisions, because the resources you have already spent are gone and can't be recovered. Just because you've worked on a project for a long time doesn't mean you can't walk away from it now. You should decide whether a project ought to continue on the basis of how likely it is to succeed from this point forward.

Research by Hal Arkes and colleagues demonstrates that people typically overvalue sunk costs. It's hard to walk away from a project on which they've already put in a lot of effort. This issue is particularly important in light of the popularity of *grit*. Angela Duckworth defines grit as a passionate persistence in an area of study, and some have argued that it's a significant determinant of success in school and business. Further research suggests that persistence reflects a high level of the core personality characteristic conscientiousness (which I discussed in chapter 5). Conscientious people often succeed at difficult tasks.

But studies by Richard Nisbett and colleagues suggest that the most successful people are good at determining when projects should be abandoned rather than continued. These individuals focus on the potential of a project as it currently stands rather than on how much effort has already been put into it. Good leaders help their teams step away from projects that are unlikely to succeed.

This reflects a related aspect of good leadership. Many organizations will put together groups to start projects, but have trouble ending one that has served its useful life. That's because some number of people devoted themselves to that project and have a strong allegiance to it. When you start a project, establish an end date for it. When that date is reached, people interested in continuing the project should have to make an argument for why further investment in it would be more valuable than putting those resources toward other things.

Big Decisions Are Not Like Small Ones

You make a lot of decisions every day. You choose what clothes to wear, what route to take to the office, and which tasks to tackle during the day. Most of your decisions fit squarely within the types of choices the cognitive brain is adapted to make. People are quite good at making decisions when they have experience with the options and can envision the consequences.

When you choose what to wear, you know your clothes pretty well. You can imagine how other people will evaluate them, and you get social feedback on what you're wearing over the course of the day, which can affect future decisions.

As you take on leadership roles, though, many choices you're asked to make will deviate from this ideal. You'll have to evaluate large-scale projects such as hiring new people, taking on a new product line, or structuring a deal in a novel way. These situations often go beyond what you've experienced directly. Envisioning the consequences can be hard—in part because of a lack of experience, in part because of the complexity of the environment itself, and in part because of uncertainty about outcomes. Furthermore, such large-scale projects will play out over a long time, so it will be difficult to track progress or to figure out which elements of the situation account for the success or failure of the venture.

You may be tempted to treat choices like this as you do all the other decisions in your life. If you've been successful with many small choices, you may believe you'll also be good at these more significant ones. But you need to find tools to help you make decisions in these settings. Learn to use financial projections and forecasting models. Learn to integrate opinions from experts who can interpret various kinds of data relevant to the decisions you're making.

You also need to become more comfortable with uncertainty. In the Star Wars movies, there's a recurring joke in which the 'droid C3PO gives the odds of success for particular actions, which Han Solo then ignores. (Spock and Kirk have a similar dynamic in *Star Trek*.) In many real-world situations, though, probabilities are the best tool we have for judging the likelihood of outcomes. Nevertheless, quite a bit of research, much of it done by Gerd Gigerenzer and colleagues, demonstrates that people aren't particularly good at reasoning from probabilities. If you're working in an environment in which many future projections are going to be expressed in terms of likelihood, you'll need to develop more comfort with choices that are expressed in degrees of uncertainty.

To prepare for these large-scale decisions, you need to do three things. First, look at the decisions that you and the leaders you admire have to make. Examine the degree to which they deviate from the kinds of choices that people make well, and begin to catalog the ones for which you'll need additional tools. Second, before you take on a leadership role, ask to observe important large-scale decisions being made so that you can learn what skills you'll need to become a better decision maker. Then find classes or seminars in which you can improve your abilities. Third, when you engage in large-scale decisions, make specific predictions about expected outcomes that will help you judge later whether the choice seems to be working well. The more indications you have that your decision is or isn't going well, the easier it will be to course-correct a big project and the better your future decisions will be.

Communicating as a Leader

Chapter 6 focused exclusively on communication. I want to pick up two related topics here, though. The first is communicating effectively about uncertainty. The second is public speaking—particularly using speeches to motivate others.

Communicating about Uncertainty

One of the most difficult issues in any organization is uncertainty about the future. In 2008, the worldwide economy took a downturn following the collapse of the housing market in the United States and the ensuing credit crunch. This event affected a number of organizations, including the University of Texas, where I work. The staff at the university was bracing for job cuts. People were trying to decide whether to look for other jobs or wait it out. Supervisors weren't sure what to say to their employees, because the upper administration was providing very little information. Its lack of communication stemmed from uncertainty about the outcome of the Texas legislature's budget debate, which made it hard to predict what cuts (if any) would need to be made.

When faced with this kind of uncertainty, it's tempting to say nothing at all. You don't have anything valuable to add to the conversation, so it might seem like a good strategy to wait until you have more information before talking with people.

However, people think a lot about stressful situations. In the absence of information from you, they'll generate all kinds of scenarios for the future, and they'll talk about those scenarios with one another. As the stories spread, they'll begin to take on their own reality. Once a story takes root—even if it isn't based on any facts—it's hard to dislodge it from people's memories. Research by Hollyn Johnson and

Colleen Seifert on the *continued influence effect* demonstrates that it's quite difficult to get people to stop using information they've heard in the past, even when they know the information is false. So a communication vacuum will be filled by the stories people tell one another, and those stories will persist.

That means you need to communicate about uncertain events, even if all you can say is that you don't yet have any information that will help predict what's going to happen. If the people you work with trust that you're transparent, they may still speculate about the future, but they're less likely to generate an elaborate web of beliefs about what's actually going on.

JAZZ BRAIN:
Listen More Than You Play

One of the first things jazz musicians learn when they start to play with others is something I call The First Law of Jazz. Whenever you sit in with a new combo, you should listen more than you play.

Any skilled performance involves more than simply executing some procedure. Playing effectively with other musicians means playing *with* them, not just *near* them. You cannot be influenced by their style or their innovations if you don't listen first. Similarly, you cannot expect to be a good leader if you don't listen to your colleagues, clients, and customers. They can tell you a lot about what they like and don't like.

Listening doesn't mean doing what other people say. But you cannot communicate as a leader if you don't know what other people want and what they're thinking about. You have to find a way to connect your ideas and suggestions to what they already know and believe. As a new leader, you may feel pressure to do something quickly. But your long-term success depends on your willingness to really hear what's going on around you.

Speaking to Groups

When you take on a leadership role, you often have to get up in front of groups to speak. Public speaking is one of the top social stressors. It is so difficult for so many people that it's routinely used to create stress in psychology experiments. Participants are told, for example, that they have ten minutes to prepare a speech they'll present to experts who will evaluate their performance. These instructions reliably lead to an increase in people's stress levels and to the release of stress hormones.

The best way to reduce your stress around public speaking is to give talks. This is a version of *exposure therapy*, pioneered by Michael Telch and colleagues, that is used to reduce stress, anxiety, and fear around many phobias. The principle of exposure therapy is to face the thing you fear without doing anything designed to "protect" you from bad outcomes, such as taking a pill or wearing your lucky shoes. Over time, your motivational brain learns that the experience doesn't lead to a bad outcome, so your anxiety is reduced.

To ensure that you don't have a bad outcome when giving a public speech, you need to practice. It may seem silly, but public speaking is a performance, and every performer needs to rehearse. After your speech is written (or outlined, depending on your preference for giving remarks), find a quiet place and deliver it to a wall a few times. Use the same volume and the same intensity you would for the actual occasion. Practice speaking clearly, enunciating your words, and pause in the right places to give the desired impact. If you need feedback, find a trusted colleague or consider hiring a speech coach to listen to you and recommend ways to improve.

You might take a lesson from the world of stand-up comedy. Comedians use a lot of metaphors about death when talking about their craft. Having a great set means *killing* the audience. Having a terrible set involves *dying* onstage. As bad as it must feel to tell jokes that fall flat in front of a crowd that wants to laugh, great comedians are willing to take the chance again and again that they will die onstage. With all that practice, they realize that dying isn't so bad after all. And they use the bad experiences to improve their performance in the future rather than allowing setbacks to keep them from trying again.

For leaders, an important function of public speaking is to build engagement for a project. Research by Jack Brehm and Elizabeth Self on the intensity of motivation suggests that people are most highly motivated to achieve goals when they're aware of a gap between the present and a desired future and they have a plan they believe will bridge that gap. That is, when there is a *bridgeable gap*. A good motivational speech highlights those elements. You have to help your audience recognize where they are right now and what the future can look like. Then you need to describe how their actions can bring the desired future into being. It's also valuable to acknowledge the obstacles they may face and recognize that those barriers can be overcome.

You don't need to be an energetic speaker to share a vision of the future with the people you work with. You just need to speak with confidence about how the group can succeed by working together. To see a wonderful example of a motivational speech, watch the first scene of the movie *Patton*, in which George C. Scott portrays the general in an Oscar-winning performance. You can watch it on You-Tube. In that scene, General Patton is speaking to the Third Army just before it invades France. He does an excellent job of highlighting the situation and reminding the troops of the strength of the US Army tradition. What makes the speech particularly powerful, though, is that Patton tells the men that they're likely to be afraid when under enemy fire and seeing their fellow soldiers being killed. He exhorts them to keep fighting despite that fear. By laying out a vision and a plan along with potential obstacles, he is preparing the young soldiers for battle.

Personal Responsibility

People in leadership positions have an outsize influence on their organizations. They can set a vision and galvanize people to work toward it. As a result, they often get disproportionate credit for an organization's successes.

It can be challenging to adjust to this. Early in your career, you have to do a lot to ensure that your contributions will be noticed and that you'll be considered for new opportunities. Once you're in a leadership role, though, the spotlight is already on you. Even if you hope to continue advancing in the organization, you don't need to bring attention to yourself. Instead, you need to focus on developing the people who work for you.

That means that when something goes wrong in your group, you must be willing to accept the blame and shield your people from consequences they might face from those higher up in the organization. You can work to fix the problem within your group, and you may choose to punish someone for negligence. But that doesn't need to be broadcast beyond the group. Your team's performance is your responsibility, and you need to own that. You should protect your employees, because someone who makes a mistake today may develop into a star tomorrow. You don't want to ruin that person's reputation with other leaders in the organization.

The opposite holds true for credit. As the leader of the team, you'll get a lot of credit when things go well. You rarely need to toot your own horn. You should highlight the work of people who were instrumental in the success of a venture.

Consider two reasons to broadcast your team's accomplishments. First, the higher up you move in an organization's food chain, the more your performance will be judged according to your ability to develop the talents of others. If you can demonstrate that you have a positive impact on the people who work for you, others will notice, and you'll be given more opportunities to lead.

Second, as you rise in an organization, you'll need allies to help you implement projects that interest you. A great way to develop loyalty within an organization is to aid people on your team in advancing their careers. Those who can attribute some of their success to you are likely to support your future efforts.

In the context of developing future leaders, think about how to promote diversity in a leadership team. As discussed in chapter 7, diverse teams often generate creative solutions to problems. Yet in many organizations, the higher up you go, the less diverse the leadership is. Part of the problem—at least in studies of people from the United States and Western Europe—is that leadership behaviors are evaluated more positively in men than in women and in white people than in people of color. So the people selected for additional leadership training and opportunities tend to be white males.

Every leader should look for chances to provide leadership opportunities and training to all an organization's employees and to promote people on the basis of their performance rather than on judgments of leadership potential. Organizations should recognize that the people who are best qualified for positions later in their careers often had significant opportunities to develop those qualifications early on.

Quiet Leadership

Because leaders are expected to set an organization's strategic agenda, people often focus on their broad pronouncements about the future. As a result, leaders are often judged on the basis of those statements. But an organization's success is strongly driven by operational factors. Vision is important for setting direction, but vision alone won't make the organization reach its goals.

Quiet leadership, in which people work behind the scenes to uphold the quality of the organization's endeavors, is commonly undervalued. Quiet leadership involves teaching colleagues how to improve their performance. It involves holding everyone to a high standard. It involves paying attention to the details of how things are done.

I've been to a number of meetings over the years in which people have discussed projects and solicited feedback from the group. Even when the group is lukewarm about an idea, a few people make comments, and the team moves forward with the project. In private discussions, people talk about their misgivings, but nobody actually raises those issues when there's a chance to do something about them.

Not long ago, though, I was in a meeting with many high-level administrators at my university. Someone presented a plan for identifying potential future risks for the university. The plan was OK, but it seemed to omit a number of key opportunities to identify new risks. One administrator, who was hearing this proposal for the first time, immediately made a number of specific recommendations for improving the plan. Those at the meeting could easily have let the plan move forward, and the person who spoke up was doing so in a small forum away from most of the university. But that moment of quiet leadership was a great demonstration of holding high standards for work within an organization.

You don't need to be in a position of authority to engage in quiet leadership. If you believe a project can be improved, say so. Early in your career, you may be uncomfortable criticizing something in a public meeting, but you can always engage someone later by email or in a private conversation.

The central element of quiet leadership is being constructive. It's not enough just to look for a proposal's limitations; you must work with others to develop alternatives. Quiet leaders find ways to teach others what they know to enhance the capabilities of everyone in an organization.

People who routinely work constructively to improve projects and to develop the skills of people around them are noticed. They're the ones everyone ultimately wants on the team for an important project. And when someone is on many different teams whose projects succeed, people notice what those teams have in common.

Fostering Collaboration

As discussed in chapter 7, workplaces function best when colleagues treat one another like neighbors. That is, they develop trust and settle up the debts in the long run. That means colleagues will do favors for one another without expecting immediate reciprocity.

Leaders should look for signs that the neighborhood isn't functioning well and identify ways to improve it. The neighborhood may break down in two ways. One possibility—the most common—is that the workplace becomes less trusting, and colleagues become more like strangers. The other is that it becomes more like a family, with no checks and balances on whether particular individuals are being productive.

When employees start focusing solely on carrying out the duties they've been asked to accomplish, rather than looking for ways to contribute more broadly to the mission of the organization, you can feel that the workplace is becoming a collection of strangers. When people wait to be asked to work on a project rather than engaging, they are demonstrating that they view their work as a series of fee-for-service transactions. Such workplaces have a high level of turnover, because people are looking for a better environment.

Chances are, when people treat their colleagues as a collection of strangers, it's because they don't believe that the organization is fulfilling its end of the bargain to create a neighborhood. It's important to sit down with them and discuss their frustrations with colleagues, management, or even your own leadership. They may feel they're not being fairly compensated for their work, or that their contributions aren't being recognized. Differences between their compensation and that of upper management may create a sense of unfairness. One reaction to unfairness is to pull out of the neighborhood.

After you've identified what makes people feel like strangers, you need to respond. If aspects of your own leadership behavior are pushing them away, seek mentorship and coaching to help you regain their trust. If other things about the organization are driving people away from the neighborhood, you need to advocate visibly for your direct reports. You also need to make them aware of your interest in their careers. Your efforts to develop their knowledge and skills will make them feel like valued members of the community.

Some organizations want everyone to feel part of a family. The problem with that is that it makes people less likely to be held accountable for shoddy work or missed assignments. The family model works well when an organization needs to take care of an employee who is sick or going through a difficult time; but in the workplace itself, people should maintain the attitude that everyone has to contribute and that those who take more than they give will not succeed. As a leader, you must be serious about regular performance reviews and make it clear that people will be recognized for good performance, but everyone is expected to be a significant contributor.

Much of this rests on a sense of honor in the workplace. My colleague Paul Woodruff, in his wonderful book *The Ajax Dilemma*, points out that disparities in pay or observations that some people work hard while others are loafing take an emotional toll on employees. When people feel that their contributions aren't respected, they question the organization's commitment to them. This leads to frustration and anger, which will ultimately weaken their commitment to the organization.

The Dual-Relationship Principle

In chapter 1, I mentioned a woman who had difficulty maintaining her friendships with colleagues after she was promoted to a supervisory role. Such a transition is hard on relationships because of what's called the *dual-relationship principle*.

Clinical psychologists have a therapeutic relationship with their clients and are ethically barred from having any other kind. They cannot be friends with their patients or be in romantic relationships with them, and they cannot treat family members or business partners. This principle stems from the recognition that each relationship you have with someone has different goals. A therapeutic relationship requires trust so that the patient can disclose information, but it also requires that the therapist be able to give feedback that the patient may find difficult to hear. To ensure that nothing takes primacy over the therapeutic relationship, therapists must avoid any other kind of relationship with their patients.

In the workplace, however, the dual-relationship principle is not an ironclad ethical rule. It's reasonable for supervisors to have social relationships with their reports, and lots of workplace romances work out just fine. But when you become a supervisor for the first time, you should recognize that the goals of your new position may conflict with some of the goals related to being friends with your peer group when you started work. Your new role may create some tension or complications that you need to navigate. You may want to set ground rules about the conversations you have in social settings so that office gripes don't become interpersonal battles when you're out having fun.

Have explicit conversations with people you work with if you're concerned about how your work relationship is affecting your personal relationships. Initiating these conversations may be awkward, because people don't generally talk about boundaries in their social lives. But when work and social life collide, as they often do, it can be useful to ensure that everyone is comfortable with the constraints that may come from potentially conflicting goals.

Ethical Behavior

A final aspect of leadership involves ethics. The tools of leadership are value-neutral. Over the course of history, we have celebrated leaders for doing things that made the world a better place and reviled leaders who caused suffering and harm to others.

The trade-off between options that have short-term benefits and those that do good in the long term has ethical implications for leaders. The *shareholder value* ideology for running publicly traded corporations, for example, often pits short-term decisions that affect the quarterly stock price against long-term benefits to the company and its employees. There is no "correct" answer to dilemmas that involve these trade-offs. Instead, leaders must turn to values to guide how they approach them.

This leads to another wonderful distinction Woodruff makes in *The Ajax Dilemma*—between *ideals* and their *doubles*. An ideal is some standard that you want to live up to. For example, you might want to lead in a *just* manner that allows people to be recognized for their achievements and rewards them accordingly. A value's double is a procedure that's applied uncritically in an attempt to create that ideal. The typical double for justice is *fairness*. When you treat everyone in the same way, you don't have to think critically about each situation; instead, you can apply a rule. Even if the outcome is bad, it's easy to justify, because it follows a preset rule that was based on an easily articulated principle.

For most organizations, it wouldn't be feasible to have every manager think through solutions to potential ethical dilemmas in the workplace. For one thing, individual-level decision making can be time-consuming. For another, it can lead to inconsistencies across the organization that may hamper productivity. So organizations design procedures for approaching these ideals to ensure a consistency of outcomes across organizational units. Unfortunately, these procedures often lead to suboptimal outcomes.

If you find yourself in a leadership position in which you must enforce policies whose outcomes conflict with your values or have consequences that violate the organization's ideals, you should speak up. In many cases, policies were initially implemented with good intentions but nevertheless cause problems. You may have to enforce a bad policy in the short term, but that's not sustainable in the long term.

It's important to point out the negative consequences of policies to higher-level leaders in the organization. Often they don't have direct experience with how procedures are being implemented and what effect they are having. By speaking up, you can spur policy revisions that will do a better job of upholding the organization's ideal. In addition, if you let the people you supervise know that you're working to change policies that have unjust outcomes, you can maintain trust with them while still adhering to the workplace rules your position requires you to implement.

Of course, if a bad policy remains in place even after you've tried to get it changed, you should question whether you want to continue working for that organization. I return to this issue in chapter 9.

THE TAKEAWAYS

Your Brains

Motivational Brain

- People are sensitive to what's being rewarded in the environment.
- People often adopt the goals of those around them through goal contagion.
- Motivational intensity reflects bridgeable gaps—some difference between present and future for which there is a plan to minimize or eliminate that difference.

Social Brain

- Charismatic leaders value the strategic components of leadership over the operational ones.
- Having multiple relationships with an individual creates conflicts of interest among those relationships.

Cognitive Brain

- Learning is error-driven.
- People place value on *sunk costs* in decision making.
- People have difficulty reasoning about probabilities.
- The *continued influence effect* means that information discovered to be false can continue to affect judgments.

Your Tips

- Learn to think both strategically and operationally.
- Good leaders teach their supervisees how to do tasks; you cannot delegate tasks otherwise.
- There is what you say, what you do, and what you reward, and people notice those in reverse order. When people don't do what

you ask them to, it's probably because of a misalignment between what's being said, what people are doing, and what's being rewarded.

- Punish negligence, not failure.
- Learn to say yes *and* to say no, and when you say no, understand your reasons.
- Learn to make decisions on the basis of statistics and probabilities.
- Communicate often with the people you lead, even if you have to tell them that the future is uncertain.
- When you take on a leadership role, listen.
- Work on your public speaking skills. Practice a lot. Don't worry too much about bad talks.
- Learn to highlight bridgeable gaps in motivational talks.
- Be aware of the *dual-relationship principle*.
- Develop a personal ethos that you can bring to your leadership.
- Recognize that procedures may lead to outcomes that don't reflect your ideals.

PART THREE

Managing Your Career

9

Move Away, Move On, or Move Up

Your career is more than just one job—it reflects the contributions you make over a lifetime of work. What you hope to contribute may well change over time. We certainly don't expect people to take the career paths they envision at age five, or even during adolescence. But you shouldn't hold your forty-year-old self to the wishes of your twenty-five-year-old self either.

About once a year, take stock of where you are in your work life and think about how your career trajectory aligns with the contributions you want to make and with your overall career and life goals. This will help you address three core questions about moving forward. Is this the career path for me, or should I *move away*? Am I dissatisfied with my organization, and should I try to *move on*? Is it time for me to take on new responsibilities, and should I *move up*? These questions will be the focus of this chapter.

Whether you stay in a particular job, of course, is not always your choice. Employers may downsize, eliminating your job; companies are bought or go bankrupt. Your employer may decide you're not a good fit in your job and fire you. The questions explored in this chapter are relevant to you anyway. I'll take up getting a new job after losing one in chapter 10.

Should I Move Away?

Career decisions are bets about the future that rest on three components. First, you're predicting that the career you choose will provide a desirable work-life balance along with the financial resources to achieve your personal goals. Second, you're betting that this career will allow you to have the impact in the world that you desire. Third, you're expecting that the day-to-day work you do and the environment in which you choose to do it will be fulfilling. You must evaluate these three areas when deciding whether to stay on your career path.

Your Lifestyle

It's hard to predict what you'll want in the future. Research on *attitude-behavior consistency* going back to Icek Ajzen and Martin Fishbein in the 1970s suggests that people often mispredict what they will want in the future, whether for small things (such as ice cream flavors) or big ones (such as career paths). That's because they're rarely in the same motivational state in the future that they were in when they made the prediction.

Some studies even show that people are poor at judging how good or bad they'll feel after achieving or failing to achieve key career goals. In one study, Dan Gilbert and Tim Wilson asked college professors up for tenure how they would feel six months after the decision if they did or did not get it. Faculty members who get tenure can basically keep their jobs for life, so it's a momentous decision. As you might expect, the professors predicted that they would be much happier six months after getting tenure than six months after being denied it. The researchers followed up with their subjects six months after the tenure decisions, and found that people were about equally happy either way.

So you can be forgiven for being unable to forecast how various aspects of your life will influence your feelings about your job. And of course you cannot predict future events, even if you're exactly right about what you want from life. Denise was a college professor with significant teaching and research responsibilities. She and her husband adopted children, who turned out to require a lot more attention than expected because of medical problems. She negotiated to take a less demanding academic position for a while in order to spend more time with her children. Such decisions have consequences for the future. Even though Denise continued to publish papers during this period of reduced workload, her department wouldn't allow her to return to the tenure-track position she had previously occupied. She and her husband eventually moved to another university. Once again, circumstances beyond your control may affect your career path.

The first question in your yearly evaluation should be whether you're happy with how your career integrates with the rest of your life. What do you think about your financial rewards? As the director of the Human Dimensions of Organizations program, I've worked with many people who devoted their early careers to the nonprofit sector but ultimately needed to find better-paying jobs. As much as they valued their organizational missions, these individuals were unable to support families on the salaries in that sector, so they chose to move away.

The second question should be whether your job permits the work-life balance you want. After adopting children, Denise elected to take a less demanding job. I've seen the reverse occur. Some musicians

I know took jobs primarily to pay the bills early in their careers so that they could devote time to music; later they prioritized jobs outside the music industry and made music their hobby.

Discovering that your current career path meets neither your financial nor your personal goals doesn't necessarily mean that you'll want to step away from it. But you should be realistic about whether that path will permit any changes in your future work-life balance. If not, you'll either continue to be disappointed or you'll need to change something significant about your work.

Your Contribution

Another facet of your work that may be causing you dissatisfaction is the contribution you're making. It's common to have high hopes early in your career for what you can accomplish. Not every job you take will enable sufficient progress in that direction.

I spoke with a friend of mine from high school whose story provides an excellent example. After getting an undergraduate degree in physics, Bob went to work for a company that made research instruments. The company was acquired and then merged with other companies. Bob was put in charge of some research and development teams, but the company often wanted him to train new groups in other countries so that it could outsource jobs to locations with more-favorable tax laws. Ultimately, Bob felt stuck in middle management. He couldn't influence high-level decisions within the organization, but he couldn't see whole projects through to completion either. One day, after getting an MRI on his back following an injury, he began to think that working as an imaging technician would be more rewarding than what he was doing, even though the field was less lucrative. He ultimately got certified as an X-ray tech. Because of his background in physics and instrumentation, he was also able to teach in certification programs and correspond with textbook authors about how imaging is taught. He doesn't make as much money as he did in his previous career, but he loves going to work.

Perhaps your skills and opportunities won't allow you to make the contribution you'd like to. As a PhD adviser, I work with many students who enter graduate school with the dream of becoming college professors. In the United States, we produce many more PhDs in most domains than there are entry-level academic jobs. Toward the end of a graduate career, students can judge whether they might be successful in the academic job market. Many of them elect to look for jobs where they can use their research skills in companies.

Your priorities may also change over time. Jay made a decision to change careers. He worked for a company that did research for financial firms looking to evaluate investment opportunities. During his tenure there, the company grew, and he shared in that success. In his forties he got cancer, and while he was undergoing treatment, he reflected on his career. He started a blog to share those thoughts and the importance of having a vocation rather than just a job (as I discussed in chapter 2). The treatments were ultimately successful. Soon after he returned to work, though, he was offered a chance to separate from the company, which he seized. Jay recognized that he wanted more meaning from his work and ultimately chose to look for a different path.

Your Process

When you choose a career path, you're making an assumption about the activities you'll enjoy in the future. As a young person, you might like the challenge of developing a new client and the excitement of traveling around a region to visit with prospects, so you'll relish the opportunities in a sales job with a national company. You might have a lot of success in the job. What you can't know is how much you'll *continue* to enjoy working with new clients and traveling frequently.

Maybe that lifestyle will be thrilling for your entire career. But maybe you will tire of airplanes, chain hotels, and dinners on an expense account.

Losing your passion for the tasks and pace of your work is often called *burnout*. A vicious cycle develops. You don't enjoy the outcomes of the work you're doing, so you experience negative emotions related to work such as stress, sadness, and frustration. Those feelings make you less resilient to bad things that happen at work, so your negative emotions increase. Eventually, you may come to dislike both the tasks you have to perform and the people you deal with at work—your colleagues and your clients. It becomes harder to motivate yourself to go to work and to give your best while you're there.

Not all cases of burnout require a career change, of course. You can engage in several strategies to increase your resilience. For example, meditation and other mindfulness techniques help decrease stress and anxiety by slowing down your reactions to stressors in the workplace. You may then feel better about the work you're doing and have more energy to overcome adversity.

Your resilience may increase if you have close colleagues at work. When you like the people you work with, your job feels like a team effort, so you're not facing problems alone. You can also do fulfilling things outside work, such as spending time with family and friends, hobbies, or exercise. Feeling burned out isn't a reason to throw in the towel on your career—but it is a sign that you should do something different. The lack of motivation and emotional fatigue that come with burnout are unlikely to get better on their own.

In the modern workplace, people don't use all their vacation time. Most employers provide paid time off, but they can't force you to use it. Some people feel that if they avoid vacation, they'll be viewed as diligent and will be put on the fast track for promotion. But nobody really pays attention to that kind of sacrifice, so there's little upside to stockpiling your vacation time.

There *is*, however, a big downside. Time away from work is important—to sleep late, visit a foreign city, hike in the mountains, or read for pleasure. Days away from work also provide perspective on the problems you're facing in the workplace, which can loom large in your emotional world if you deal with them daily. Your motivational brain will cause you to focus on them all the time. Taking a break from work helps your motivational brain disengage from these work problems, so you can reprioritize the issues you think are central. Regular vacations should become a part of your toolbox for maintaining resilience. And there's some evidence that if you're really struggling at work, a very long vacation—more than fourteen days—will have a bigger long-term impact on your well-being than a week or less.

If you've tried hard to increase your resilience and you still deeply dislike your work tasks, it may be time to consider a career change. However, as I discussed in chapter 2, your enjoyment of your work comes in part from the tasks themselves, but also from how much you can connect it to a larger mission. As you look for other career opportunities, notice when an organization's mission resonates with your values. Ideally, your next career will provide particular tasks that you like and also an opportunity to contribute in an area that's important to you.

Can You Really Change Careers?

Deciding that a career change would be ideal is not the end of the process. Chances are, you've encountered many people who hate their jobs but don't make a move. Acting on a decision to change careers requires support from people around you along with a plan for the future.

You probably need your income. You may be supporting family members as well as yourself. A career switch requires that you talk to those family members about what is feasible. Can you afford to take time away from work to retrain? Can you afford the additional schooling that may be required to pursue a new career? Can you afford to start toward the bottom of the food chain in a new organization? In the conversation with Bob that I mentioned earlier, he told me that it had been easier for him to choose a less lucrative career because he and his wife had elected not to have children.

You may find that your answer to some of those questions is no. In that case, you should focus on the resilience skills described in the previous section to make the work you're doing as bearable as possible.

As I mentioned at the very beginning of this book, though, switching career paths is becoming more common. Making a change now carries less stigma than it did thirty years ago. That means you have less to justify to potential employers than did career-switching workers in the past.

Simply deciding to make a career change doesn't mean you have to quit your current job. If your desired new career requires new skills, consider taking classes or pursuing another degree while continuing to work. About a quarter of the students in the Human Dimensions of Organizations master's program at the University of Texas are looking to make some kind of career transition. Many of them switch careers only after receiving their degrees. Jeannie took that path. She enrolled in the program with the intention of changing careers, and within six months of graduating, she had landed a job that she described in a social media post as "the best job ever."

Another option is to work with a career coach to identify what skills you need to be a good candidate for your desired position. You can then take the time to shore up any weaknesses to smooth your transition. This is particularly important if your new career path requires a license or certification.

You may be tempted to keep your plans a secret at your current workplace. And you may be right to do so. If you believe the organization would not be supportive—or might even find reasons to let you go—keep your efforts under wraps.

But divulging your plans to colleagues can have advantages. For one thing, your attitude toward the work you're doing may improve, because you know it's temporary. A big source of frustration in any situation is the lack of a feeling of *agency*. If you feel you don't have control over your circumstances, your resilience and motivation decrease. When you seize control over your future career, you may find that the frustrations of your current work diminish.

In addition, your colleagues may be more supportive of your desire to change jobs than you think. If one of them was thinking of changing careers, chances are you'd want the best for that person. Your colleagues will probably feel the same way. And they may have people in their networks who could help you establish your new career.

Should I Move Up?

A key decision point in any career is whether to seek advancement. This may not seem your choice to make, because we tend to look at careers in terms of promotions. The concept of a *dead-end job* assumes that if you're not in a position to move up in an organization, you're wasting your time. This section examines the prospects for moving up in an organization. I begin with considerations about whether to advance and then explore strategies for finding positions.

Deciding to Advance

At the outset, you should distinguish between career *development* and career *advancement*. Career development involves learning new skills and knowledge relating to your work and trying new things. It's possible to develop even in the absence of opportunities to advance.

For example, suppose you opened a coffee shop in your neighborhood. You own it, so you don't really have an opportunity to "advance." But you might run that shop for thirty years, during which time you'll learn new skills in how you present your offerings to customers and how you work with, motivate, and train employees. That sounds like a fulfilling career, despite the absence of any promotions.

If you're thinking about whether to move up, start by finding out what opportunities for career development are available to you. As discussed in chapter 5, take advantage of classes, funds for outside training, and mentoring. Talk with supervisors and mentors about skills you might need for advancement. Find ways to develop those skills while you're in your current job. Not only will that speed your path to a new position, but it will demonstrate the kind of initiative that organizations often look for when selecting candidates for promotion.

Of course, don't look ahead too quickly. You must ensure that you're doing your current job well. Early in their careers, people may be impatient to move on to jobs with more responsibility or prestige. The current job may feel less important than what they could be doing in a more advanced role, so they may not pay attention to the details of their work. But higher-level positions in an organization's hierarchy often require an understanding—and sometimes mastery—of the skills of lower-level positions.

Advancement in organizations is of two kinds—technical and managerial. Some technical jobs, and sometimes technical tracks within organizations, give you more responsibility for executing tasks. In an entry-level sales job, you're probably responsible for a small number of clients and have more oversight from experienced sellers. In a senior position, your territory or region will increase. Microsoft has a technical ladder for skilled programmers and engineers that allows them to take on more responsibility for projects within their area of expertise.

Your firm may not have a long technical career ladder, but it almost certainly has a management track. People often go from entry-level positions, in which their day-to-day responsibilities rest on a particular skill set and expertise, to supervisory positions, in which they do less technical work and more operational work. In the past, the assumption has been that a leader's or a manager's effectiveness is distinct from that person's technical expertise. For example, a typical MBA program brings in students in their middle to late twenties. It's rarely possible to have developed significant technical expertise in a domain by that age. If management requires a separate set of skills, getting an advanced degree to jump on the management track makes sense.

More-recent work suggests that good leaders and managers generally do have technical skills in their areas of expertise. It's hard to envision what strategies can be implemented absent a reasonable knowledge of the organization's specific goals. It's difficult to mentor people if you don't clearly understand their job and how it's done. So those who aspire to a people-management track need to develop technical skills and to pay attention to exactly how things are accomplished within the organization.

The next question you should address in your approach to advancement is the time commitment. Promotions entail added responsibilities, which will require both more of your actual time and more of your mental time. The job may involve late meetings, travel, or other commitments that will extend your working hours and perhaps give you less flexibility in those hours than you have now. Rarely does advancement lead to a reduction in work time.

Advancement also makes your job more mentally taxing during your nonworking hours. You will be asked to address thorny problems—business issues that need to be thought through, or interpersonal problems that must be addressed. You might even need to deal with issues related to the physical plant of your business. Vivian moved into a director-level position in her organization and in her third week in the role, she was awakened by a phone call about nasty graffiti scrawled on the exterior of the office building. She had to coordinate with building maintenance staff as well as the local police before settling into her work day.

Either way, research in the 1920s by Bluma Zeigarnik and Maria Ovsiankina demonstrates that when you're struggling with a problem, your motivational brain ensures that problem remains active in your cognitive brain, and so you'll continue thinking about it even after the workday is over. You need to be prepared that the higher you advance, the likelier it is that work will stay lodged in your memory whether you want it to or not.

The last major consideration when thinking about advancement is salary. Often this is one of the first things people think about. You probably share the general assumption that wages (and buying power) will continue to rise as your career progresses. Dissatisfaction with pay frequently drives people to think about getting a promotion. I've put this last on the list, though, because salary isn't a good driver of long-term happiness or work satisfaction. Research on the *hedonic treadmill* suggests that increases in happiness from raises or promotions are fleeting once basic needs for food, clothing, and shelter have been addressed. Although a raise gives you a short-term boost in happiness and satisfaction, you adapt to the new level of income after a few months and then start looking forward to the next raise or promotion.

If you're not excited by the mission and tasks that a new position entails, no amount of money will make it fulfilling. You're better off adapting your lifestyle to your income than seeking a job that will provide the level of income you currently desire.

That said, if you've been in your position for a while, you may feel that you deserve more money than you're making. Perhaps you see disparities in what people in your office are paid. Perhaps competing firms pay more for similar jobs. Perhaps living expenses are high in your region, and you're struggling to make ends meet. Any of these situations can be a good reason to talk to your supervisor or the HR department about getting a raise.

It can be uncomfortable to advocate for yourself, particularly if you're high in agreeableness, which makes you want to be liked by other people. You may have trouble asking for things because you worry about how others will react to your requests. A study by Timothy Judge, Beth Livingston, and Charlice Hurst found that people who are relatively low in agreeableness tend to make more money (on average) than people who are relatively high in agreeableness—though the former are also more likely to get fired.

If you have concerns about your salary, it's important to raise them. Those concerns can fester over time, making you dissatisfied with your organization and likely to seek employment elsewhere. And even if your firm gives you an unasked-for raise, it may be less than you hoped for. Your employers cannot read your mind. If you want or believe you deserve something, you should ask for it so that they can meet your needs or at least talk to you about what's possible.

If you do meet to discuss a raise, do your homework ahead of time. First, make sure you know who can authorize the raise. It's not always your supervisor. Second, if you're concerned about what others at your company are earning, be certain that your information is correct. You don't want to accuse your employer of underpaying you on the basis of rumors that turn out to be false. If you think you're underpaid relative to other people in your industry, look at industry averages for your experience level to document that. The better prepared you are for the meeting, the better the case you can make for yourself.

Satisfaction and Dissatisfaction

How can you manage your motivation related to a promotion? You may really want one, but your manager says you have to wait a little longer to be eligible. Or you may recognize that the time is right to seek a promotion but not really be motivated to advance. What can you do?

In chapter 8, I talked about the role of bridgeable gaps in creating motivation. Studies suggest that the same principle applies when thinking about moving up in an organization. The trick is to create satisfaction when you want to stay in your job awhile and dissatisfaction when you want to push yourself to move up. This strategy is related to the one I suggested earlier in this chapter for remaining upbeat when you have to stay on a career path you don't enjoy.

You can create satisfaction by focusing on your accomplishments in your current role. Contemplate what you've done well, whom you've helped, and how you've contributed to the mission of the organization. Those thoughts will help you appreciate your current job and feel good about what you're doing.

You can create dissatisfaction by focusing on what you haven't yet accomplished in your career. Consider the contributions you still want to make but won't be able to make in your current position. Think about tasks you have to do that you wish were someone else's responsibility. These thoughts will make you less happy with your current job and help motivate you to consider alternatives.

Bear in mind that it's hard to be really satisfied with what you're doing and also motivated to seek something new.

Finding New Positions

From the first day you work at a firm, you should be paying attention to other positions there. You have good reasons to internalize the org chart. You can be more effective at getting what you want if you know whom to ask to support a project or to get resources and if you understand how decisions are made. And as you learn about the jobs that other people do, you can contemplate alternative career paths.

In chapter 5, I discussed mentorship. In many mentoring relationships, others give you advice about how to engage with your work. Just listening to other people around your organization talk about their day-to-day work life can also be valuable—it may provide a model for different ways to advance in your career. You might become aware of options that you would find exciting. (Sometimes, of course, you may learn that a job you imagined would be perfect has elements you'd be ill suited for.)

Give your network a chance to help you find the next position that would be best for you. People who are impressed with the work you've done are often interested in helping you reach your goals. But they're unlikely to offer something spontaneously, so let them know if you're interested in moving up.

Heather (a different Heather from the one whose story I told in chapter 4) has worked for more than twelve years at a large financial services firm that is interested in having people get experience in a number of different areas. So when she was ready, she let several people know she'd be interested in a new job. She said that "people came out of the woodwork" immediately to suggest positions she might take. She has used this strategy successfully every few years to find a new position within the organization.

Your network gives you a big advantage over other applicants for a position. No matter how good candidates may look on paper, it's hard for them to compete with someone who's already well known to the people doing the hiring. For one thing, those doing the hiring can envision what it will be like to work with you because they already have some experience with you. If you're invited to apply for a position, you're much more likely to be successful than if you send in an application cold.

Should I Move On?

As I've pointed out several times, it's becoming more common for people to move from one firm to another than to move up the ladder within one company. How can you decide whether your best option is to rise within your current firm or to move elsewhere?

One thing you have to consider is the availability of suitable positions in your own firm. Early in your career, you often have many options for getting promoted. But after you've risen to a certain level, it may get harder to find something in your own organization. For example, retail chains with many outlets—like Starbucks, Best Buy, and Lowe's—provide opportunities for mobility early on. People can rise through the management ranks within a particular store. After that, they may be able to get promoted to manager of a busier location. But few positions are available beyond that—say, at the district or the regional level or in the corporate home office. As a result, people with aspirations for higher-level management may have to either wait their turn for a position to open up or consider moving to another organization. Many large organizations in general have a bottleneck as people approach high-level management positions.

Jim was working for a financial services firm. He told his supervisors that he was interested in moving up into a management role. They let him know that competition was likely to be stiff for those spots and that he should expect to wait about ten years before getting a chance at the promotion he wanted. He applied for a few positions within the company to test the waters and eventually chose to move to another company that was interested in his talents.

When you're contemplating whether to stay with your organization, you should revisit your core values, which I first discussed in chapter 2. As I pointed out earlier in this chapter, your values can change over time. Your organization's values, too, may shift. Sometimes your initial perception of the values and mission of the organization may differ from the reality you experience after working there. If your personal values and those of the organization diverge, that's a good reason to consider moving to another firm that might be a better fit.

At some point in your career you may be approached by people at other organizations who are interested in recruiting you. This can happen through your social network or through recruiting firms that track successful individuals in a field and gauge their interest in moving. It can be flattering to have someone contact you out of the blue to recruit you for a position. It's always worth listening to what opportunities are out there. If you haven't really contemplated moving elsewhere, though, you might sit down with your boss and have a conversation about your future before deciding whether to pursue another possibility. Let your boss know that you're getting some interest from other firms and talk about your career aspirations. Sometimes your goals are taken more seriously when there's a real chance you might leave.

Be careful, however, to recognize what happens in your cognitive brain as you begin to think about taking a job elsewhere, whether you're being recruited or have just decided to look. You might think that you evaluate job options by weighting the information you have about each job (salary, benefits, responsibilities) and then selecting the option that has the best combination of factors. But in fact the weight you give to that information changes with your interest in the positions. As I mentioned in chapter 4, studies by Jay Russo and colleagues find that factors consistent with believing that a desired position is a good fit will become more important to you, and factors inconsistent with that belief will become less so. In other words, the emphasis you place on elements of your options starts to align with your preferences. If you're primarily interested in staying at your current firm, the benefits of staying will loom larger than the benefits of leaving. And if you're leaning toward leaving, you'll suddenly find yourself focusing on the attributes of the new position that are superior to your current situation.

This spreading coherence has two influences. First, while you're contemplating leaving your job for another, you'll feel remarkably unsettled. You'll begin to notice all the problems at your workplace, and they may start to bother you more than they did in the past. Your evaluation of your current job is being affected by the interest you have in moving.

Second, the new job may appear more attractive than it actually is. For one thing, recruiters are likely to emphasize the benefits, not the drawbacks, of working at their company.

Third, your own evaluation of the new job will be biased according to your prior work experience. To see why, let's return to the structural alignment process described in chapter 4. Recall that when you compare options, you'll emphasize alignable differences between the options (that is, elements that correspond between them) over nonalignable differences (elements that are unique to one of them). That means if the new job has a factor that you haven't encountered in your present job, you may not pay enough attention to it, leading you to overlook a drawback of the new position. You may discover after moving that you've traded one set of frustrations for another.

This way of making comparisons leads to the "grass is greener" effect. You are intimately familiar with the flaws of your current employer and unfamiliar with the problems you'll encounter at the new organization. One way to avoid being disappointed is to bear in mind that a new job is rarely as ideal as it seems when you're making a decision about whether to move. And if you do move, you should be prepared to discover problems you didn't anticipate.

This doesn't mean you should never move. It just means you should recognize that you were probably wearing rose-colored glasses when evaluating the new position.

JAZZ BRAIN:

Whose Song Is That?

In jazz, people play a lot of covers—versions of songs written and often initially recorded by someone else. A musician might learn a version of a tune in one ensemble and then move to another and perform the same song. That is generally accepted practice. (Of course, if you record and sell a song written by someone else, you have to acknowledge that and pay a royalty to the writer, often through a service like BMI or ASCAP.)

In business, though, the rules are different. Some of the things you're working on belong to you, and others belong to the organization employing you. This ownership becomes particularly important when you choose to leave a firm and take a new job.

You must grapple with both legal and ethical issues. From a legal standpoint, you should be careful both when negotiating for a job and when leaving one to understand what you own and what your firm owns. If you work in sales or another job that has clients, what legal obligation do you have to leave your client list with your current firm, and to what degree may you retain that list when you move? Consider hiring a labor attorney to look over contracts before you sign away your rights to clients and customers. And if you've developed intellectual property during your tenure with a firm, make sure you know who owns it and whether you may take any of it to a new job.

Ethically, you also want to consider your obligations both to the firm where you worked and to your customers and clients. In some professions, such as medicine and law, a practitioner's relationship with a client is deeply personal, so many professionals will alert their clients of moves to a new practice and give them the option to follow. In some sales jobs, though, you've developed customers and clients using the resources owned by the firm and with the help of the people, structures, and processes developed by that firm. Taking that property without some compensation to the firm seems like an ethical violation, even if there are no legal barriers to doing so.

THE TAKEAWAYS

Your Brains

Motivational Brain

- People mispredict the influence of negative events on their future happiness.

- Anxiety and stress make it harder to ignore negative things that happen at work.

- Having a sense of agency helps people feel good about their situation.

- Uncompleted tasks drive attention and memory, because the goal remains active.

Social Brain

- Having close colleagues at work increases resilience.

Cognitive Brain

- You can best predict your future attitude when your current situation is like the one you'll be in later.

Your Tips

- You may be dissatisfied with your career if you mispredicted what you would want later in life or if you're unable to make the contribution you hoped to make.

- Make it a priority to develop a good relationship with colleagues. It may be more important than you think.

- Take regular vacations. The work will still be there when you get back.

- If you're dissatisfied with your career path, think about the training you'll need to get another job.

- Share your plans with colleagues; they may be able to help.

- Career *development* and career *advancement* are not the same.

- Don't try to get promoted too quickly.

- Leadership requires technical expertise as well as other skills.

- Money matters, but a raise won't make you happy for long.

- Learn to ask for what you need.

- To feel good about your current position, focus on what you do well. To motivate yourself to move up, focus on what you have yet to accomplish.

- Pay attention to the jobs other people are doing to find out about opportunities.

- You may need to move in order to advance.

- Beware of *spreading coherence* effects if you start looking at other firms. They can lead to a "grass is greener" effect.

- Be aware of what you can and cannot take away from your current job if you move.

10

Your Career

At the start of this book, I talked about how hard it is to define a career. That's partly because in the cognitive brain, a career is part of what's called an *ad hoc category*. Larry Barsalou coined this term after noticing that people invent categories such as *diet foods* (celery, carrots, calorie-free soda) and *things to take out of the house if there's a fire* (children, pets, family photos). Your career falls into the category *contributions I made during my work life*.

Barsalou found that people evaluate a member of an ad hoc category according to how close it is to the ideal member of that category. This contrasts with how they judge the goodness of categories that are based on the members' shared features. In that case the comparison is to an average or a *prototype*. Consider the feature-based category *birds*. Inclusion in this category is based on the features of the average members. For most people that means small songbirds like robins and sparrows. These birds have feathers and wings; they sing, fly, and build nests. Similar birds are judged to be good examples of the category, while dissimilar ones—such as penguins and emus—are not. In contrast, think about the ad hoc category *diet foods*. The ideal diet food is tasty and has very few calories. The more a food resembles this ideal, the better it is judged to be.

People have ideas about an ideal career as well. For many, it involves a series of jobs they love in which they continue to get promoted, increasing their salary, influence, and autonomy each time. You (and others) are likely to judge the goodness of your career according to how closely it resembles this ideal.

But your career won't necessarily fit this ideal in any way—and it probably shouldn't. When it comes to managing your career, you need to be flexible in pursuing your goals. And if other people judge your career according to the ideal, you must ensure that those judgments don't unduly influence how you make decisions. What's important is that your career is excellent for you.

In this chapter, I explore a few factors that affect your ability to manage your career. I start with a discussion about how to maximize your satisfaction with it. I examine ways to develop good relationships in new workplaces or positions. Then I turn to the broader topic of managing your social network over the course of your career. Finally, I talk about how to deal with setbacks such as layoffs and demotions.

Letting Your Career Happen

In chapter 2, I talked about the dangers of editing your career (or your life story, for that matter) in the forward direction. It's hard to gauge in advance the contribution you're going to make. And being open to experience—a personality characteristic I introduced in that discussion—will allow you to consider new possibilities that come up rather than deciding in advance that they don't fit what you envision for yourself.

It's also important to be patient about the progression of your career. We live in a fast-paced world in which, if you try, you will find ample evidence that others are doing better than you are. No matter what your field is, someone else in it has made more money or had more success at a younger age than you. Your social brain engages in a lot of comparisons between yourself and other people, and the modern social media environment makes it easy to do so.

Social comparisons are of two types—upward and downward. In an upward social comparison, you compare yourself—your accomplishments, your job, your possessions, and so forth—with someone who's doing better than you on some dimension. In a downward social comparison, you're looking at someone who's doing worse.

Although it's natural to make both types of comparisons, neither is particularly helpful in managing your career. Upward social comparisons create negative emotions. When you don't measure up to the achievements of others, you feel bad about what you've done. Those comparisons may make you strive harder to achieve your goals, but usually only if the person you compare yourself with is similar to you—works at the same company or is at the same job level. The more different the person you're comparing yourself with, the less you'll feel you can achieve what they've achieved.

Downward social comparisons tend to make you feel good about what you've accomplished—but as I discussed in chapters 8 and 9, satisfaction isn't particularly motivating. These comparisons can be an easy way to boost your mood, but they won't help you manage your career.

Alternatively, self-comparison—that is, comparing your present self to your past and future selves—can be quite valuable as a motivational tool. You assume that your future self will be nearly the same as your present self except for some achievement. Generating fantasies about this future self can energize you to pursue your goals without making you feel that you should have reached them already.

Research by Junseok Chun, Joel Brockner, and David De Cremer suggests that when you're in a position to evaluate other people, they will be more motivated by comparisons of their current performance with their past performance than by comparisons of their current performance with that of other people. They will also think such evaluations are fairer than comparisons with others.

Another important element of being patient with your career trajectory is defining success in the right way. Bear in mind that while the contributions you make in your career are motivating, they aren't a sustaining definition of success. Just as you quickly adapt to increases in your salary, you quickly acclimate to a particular goal you've achieved. Although it makes you feel good to succeed at something, that good feeling quickly wears off as your success becomes simply a part of your identity.

Factors that influence your daily satisfaction are what sustains good feeling at work. As discussed in chapter 2, people who see their work as a vocation or a calling are generally happier than those who don't, in large part because each workday is infused with meaning. So a successful career should be defined in large part according to how you do your work rather than just the outcomes.

Maintain some flexibility in how you define both the outcomes and the processes you deem successful. Years ago, I was talking with a senior colleague about why another professor, a mutual friend, was so unhappy. He had published a lot of papers that were widely read and cited in the scientific community, and had an excellent job at a top-tier research university. All of these should have given this professor a lot of joy. My colleague said, "If your only goal in life is to be a chaired professor at Harvard, then unless you end up as a chaired professor at Harvard, you lose." If your definition of success is narrowly focused on a particular outcome, it may be impossible to hit the target.

If you're unhappy with your career, look at your life situation and ask yourself whether someone else in that situation would be happy. How would you think about aspects of your life if they were happening to someone else? If you think someone else would be quite happy with your situation but you aren't, examine why you're unsatisfied. If you had your heart set on a particular outcome that hasn't come to pass, it might be worth letting go of that definition of success. It may not be easy to change your criteria for success, but it can be done.

This strategy is related to Aesop's fable about the fox that leaps to get some grapes and, finding himself unable to reach them, disparages them by saying they're probably sour. The phrase "sour grapes" is usually taken as a negative. The lesson is that your inability to obtain something shouldn't make you devalue it. But if an outcome is something you can't attain, and if pining after it decreases your satisfaction with your career and perhaps even hampers your motivation, then devaluing that outcome is actually a good idea. Maybe those grapes were sour after all.

Developing Good Relationships with New Colleagues

Over the course of your career, you're likely to experience being the new person in a group a number of times. This may happen because you move from one organization to another or because you change jobs or acquire new responsibilities in your organization.

Your ability to get work done effectively often requires developing rapport with your colleagues quickly. In chapter 3, I introduced the *halo effect*, whereby other people's social brains will interpret your efforts in the most charitable light and will be more forgiving of your errors if they already have a favorable overall impression of you. So your aim when you join a new group is to integrate yourself into the neighborhood as quickly as possible. Remember that initially you'll be treated like a stranger. People won't yet know whether they can rely on you, so you need to demonstrate that you're trustworthy.

To do that, you must first watch what people are doing and get to know what neighborly behavior in your new group looks like. Some groups prize individuals who are visibly eager to take on new tasks and to help others. Other groups dislike too much overt enthusiasm even when everyone in them is committed to organizational success. Still others have a highly competitive spirit and regard a certain amount of aggressive posturing as a sign of being part of the team. Pay attention to the social norms of your new group so that you'll be ready to contribute in a way that your colleagues appreciate.

You also need to gain trust in a way that's appropriate to the position you've taken on. If you're entering the group in a relatively low-level position, focus on completing the tasks you're given. Ask for help with jobs that are unfamiliar. If you find yourself without an obvious next task to perform, ask for suggestions about how you can help out. Don't just wait for others to come to you with requests.

If you have more supervisory responsibility for a group, gain trust by listening to people's concerns and promising to do only what you can actually accomplish. The people who work for you want to know whether you'll direct energy at the things you agree to do. They want to see you advocate with people higher up in the organization for the positions you take. They also want to know that you're consistent about what you don't agree to do. Invariably, some people will complain about your decisions. Everyone is watching to see whether complainers get more of what they want than do people who accept your decisions. Your ability to communicate transparently about your decisions will create trust in the group. And your willingness to go to bat for the people who work for you will ultimately be rewarded by loyalty and support for your initiatives.

As important as it is to make a good first impression, you won't always succeed. Perhaps you'll make an ill-advised remark, or show off a little too much in your desire to demonstrate your value to the group. You might overpromise and underdeliver on an early project.

It's also important to learn how to repair relationships that start off badly. The best way to do that is to address the problem head-on. It's natural to avoid talking with people with whom you have a strained relationship, and that may be a good strategy in many social situations. In the workplace, however, you need to be able to work with people even if you don't (yet) like them very much.

Set up a time to meet, either individually or in a small group, with people you aren't getting along with. Start by apologizing for what you may have done to lose their trust. A good apology has four components:

1. Start by making clear that you intend to apologize. That is, say you're sorry.

2. Clearly state what you did wrong. Vague and general assertions ("Mistakes were made") aren't enough. People want you to acknowledge what you did, because then they'll have some confidence that you know what you're trying to repair.

3. Promise that you're committed to changing your behavior so that what you did in the past won't happen again.

4. Specifically say what you will do to fix any problems created by your past actions.

Such apologies are also effective in larger settings. A high-level administrator at a university where I worked violated rules about the purchase of airline tickets when his spouse accompanied him on several work-related trips. It was a minor ethical violation, because his spouse played a role in the events, so it wasn't obvious that the purchases were inappropriate (though they did look bad when reported in the press). Nonetheless, this administrator immediately issued an apology in which he laid out exactly what had happened, took responsibility for the action, promised that it would not happen again, and repaid the money that had been spent on the tickets. As a result, he didn't suffer any long-term negative consequences for his ability to work with the community.

If you meet with people to start repairing your relationship with them, you must listen to what they have to say without getting defensive. Try to keep the conversation focused on the future. Talk about what you'll do to improve your relationship with others. If there are things you'd like your colleagues to do differently in the future, discuss those specifically. If you're new to a group, you may not yet be aware of its social norms. Asking your new colleagues to be specific about how you may have violated their expectations can be helpful when you've gotten off on the wrong foot with them.

It takes some practice to develop good relationships in new groups. Some people seem to have a natural gift for it, but others need to develop this skill. If you find that it's something you struggle with, consider finding a mentor or a coach who can suggest how better to integrate yourself into teams. You might even role-play situations with that mentor to practice handling these relationships.

Managing Your Social Network

As your career moves forward, you'll want to maintain contact with the many people you've worked with over time. Just because you're no longer part of a particular team on a daily basis doesn't mean that past colleagues are no longer part of your network.

This may seem particularly difficult after you've left one organization to work for another. After all, you probably disappointed quite a few people by leaving, even though changing organizations has become common. But in fact leaving is often not viewed as a betrayal. As evidence, the number of people who leave a firm only to come back at some time in the future is on the rise. These people even have a name—*boomerang employees*. Their ability to successfully return depends on their staying part of their former colleagues' neighborhoods, and vice versa.

Begin by emphasizing that you and the people you work with should succeed both jointly, for your organization, and individually, toward your career goals. Often, when working with colleagues, people focus primarily on their identity as members of the same firm. As a result, someone who leaves the firm is going from the in-group to an out-group. That creates distance in the relationship and weakens the desire to see former colleagues succeed.

Your cognitive brain allows you to categorize people in many different ways. Just because you or someone else has left your firm doesn't mean you cannot see former colleagues as part of your broader neighborhood. Remind yourself that your former colleagues are people you care about and that you're pleased to see them do well.

Even if you never return to an organization you've worked for in the past, you may still find a way to collaborate with that organization and the people in it. Nowadays companies often need to work with rivals to achieve large-scale goals that neither would be able to achieve alone. This is sometimes called *coopetition*.

Establishing an alliance with a rival can be difficult, particularly if you aren't sure you can trust the other firm. A lack of trust will stall the contract negotiations necessary to get such an alliance off the ground. If several people have worked for both firms, however, their history of cooperation can provide many more opportunities for coopetition. Maintaining your relationships with former colleagues may facilitate future events that benefit both your new firm and the one you left behind.

Thus you should avoid making negative comments about companies where you used to work. You may think that saying bad things about another company will ingratiate you with a new firm, but it actually causes two problems. The things you say about former colleagues may very well get back to them through the grapevine, so you risk damaging your relationships with them. And if you get a reputation for saying negative things about former colleagues, people will assume that it's only a matter of time before you start saying negative things about them, too.

Dealing with Setbacks

As you approach the end of this book, acknowledge that your career won't be a continual series of successes—even if you do everything right, try your hardest, work to correct your mistakes, help others, and maintain your neighborhood. Things will go wrong. You may get a bad performance evaluation. You may have a boss who doesn't like you no matter what you do. Your company may fail, despite the best efforts of your team. You may get caught in a bad economy and be laid off.

Remember that a career doesn't always move in one direction. You may take two steps forward and then a step back. How you deal with adversity over the course of your career can have a bigger effect on your ultimate success than how you planned for it. In this section, I examine ways to deal with the emotions of negative outcomes. Then I explore what you can learn from the bad times. Finally, I turn to facets of searching for a job after a layoff.

Grief

Even if you think that a bad event is coming at work, you're generally underprepared when it actually happens. When Ed was an assistant professor at a top-tier university, his publication record was solid, but his colleagues told him there was some chance he wouldn't get a tenured position. They encouraged him to apply for more grants and to look for offers from other universities that might bolster his case for promotion. He elected not to take their advice, and when his case was evaluated by the university, he was denied tenure. For several years afterward, he was angry and upset about this decision. Although he got a job at another university, he stopped attending professional conferences, and his research productivity declined. Despite the various warning signs, he didn't really expect the bad outcome, and he handled it poorly when it came.

A negative outcome is likely to create a tear in the narrative of your life. Your plans for an upward career trajectory have been disrupted. You may worry that family and friends will be disappointed in you.

Chances are, you've heard of the five stages of grief. These were described by Elisabeth Kübler-Ross, who interviewed patients with terminal illnesses. She found that people often experienced denial, anger, bargaining, depression, and (finally) acceptance. Not everyone goes through all these stages, but it's a common pattern for people who have experienced a significant life setback, such as the loss of a job or the disruption of a career path.

Because a job loss or a demotion disrupts your life story, you need to give yourself a chance to retell that story to make sense of it and to come to terms with what happened. Research by my University of Texas colleague Jamie Pennebaker demonstrates that people who write about difficult experiences not only experience less stress but also see a doctor less often for serious illnesses than do those who don't write about their experiences. Recognize that losing a job is significant and that you'll need to cope with it. Writing about what happened and how you feel a few times over the weeks following the loss can help you accept what happened and move forward.

You should also be as open as possible with your close family and friends about what has happened. Losing a job can produce feelings of guilt and shame. Guilt is an inward-facing emotion in which you feel bad about an action you took. Shame is an outward-facing emotion in which you feel bad about how something you did (or something that happened to you) will be perceived by other people.

You might feel shame after a job loss for two reasons. One is that you may have boasted about your job to other people, so losing it will make you lose face. If so, you'll have to engage with those people knowing that you may be judged for your earlier actions. As hard as it may be, you're best off addressing this head-on, admitting that your bragging has made your current situation worse for you. That opens up the possibility of getting emotional support from people who might not otherwise be sympathetic.

The other reason is that you may be guessing what other people's reactions to your situation are. You may feel, despite a lack of evidence, that you're being judged. If so, treat yourself with some compassion. Just as with mistakes you may make at work, you should imagine how you would react to the news that a close friend or a family member had lost a job. Remember, evaluating a personal situation as if it were happening to someone else can be helpful. You're often much more supportive of others than you are of yourself. Other people will often rally around you when you've experienced a loss. Emotional losses are much easier to bear when you bring other people into the process of grieving and moving forward than when you try to carry their weight alone.

One place the social brain kicks in here involves gender differences. For a variety of reasons, men are much less likely than women to seek support after a negative event. If you're a man and you experience a problem at work, you may have to overcome your natural tendency. And if a male friend, relative, or colleague has experienced a loss, think about reaching out to him to offer help, because he may not ask for assistance.

An important reason to acknowledge the emotional toll of a job loss is that many of the feelings you experience in grief make it hard to move forward. Being depressed, for example, can cause inaction. Anger doesn't generally lead to focusing on the future; rather, it's directed at the people or the organization responsible for the loss. By working through your grief, you'll become ready to do what you must to find a new job or career path.

Furthermore, a variety of sources provide evidence that unemployment can lead to physical and mental health problems. So it's particularly important to work with others to cope with the stress of being out of a job and to engage in healthful behaviors while you're between jobs.

Recovering

Moving forward with your career after a setback requires owning your share of responsibility for what happened and addressing any weaknesses on your part that may have contributed to the problem. You also have to be realistic about what the setback means for your career. Only then can you start looking for your next job.

Some setbacks result from something you did or could have done differently. You may have made a costly error. You may have slacked off in your attention to details. Perhaps there was friction in your relationships with colleagues. You must realistically assess how you have to improve to ensure that you won't suffer from the same outcome again in the future. Look back at your performance reviews and take seriously any negative feedback you've gotten. If you have an exit interview, come prepared with questions about exactly what you've done. Consider working with a career coach to uncover weaknesses in your knowledge and skills.

In some cases, you've done nothing wrong but you still get fired or demoted. Your organization may be downsizing or be poorly run, or you may be the victim of an economic slump. Even then, it's worth considering what you might do differently. Perhaps your industry sector is shrinking. Your job may be one that many companies are outsourcing or automating. If it's likely to disappear in the coming years, you may need to retrain to stay relevant in the economy of the future. A job loss may signal that it's time to consider alternatives and to find a degree or certificate program to acquire additional skills.

When you're forced to reconsider your career path, your cognitive brain may resist the thought of retraining. You've put a lot of time and energy into developing the expertise you already have. It will feel more comfortable to continue doing what you've done in the past than to retrain.

Contrary to the old adage, though, you can teach an old dog new tricks. Even if you're at mid-career or beyond, you can acquire skills that will allow you to change the job you do. In fact, a great way to stay mentally sharp is to keep challenging yourself to pick up new skills in your job, even if you're not currently thinking about switching careers. Once you get beyond any initial inertia, you'll probably find that you enjoy thinking about work in new ways.

You should acknowledge that a setback like this may alter your ideal career path. Ed—whose story appears at the start of this section—had to grapple with the prospect of not spending his entire career as a professor at a research-focused university. His career was not going to progress as he had envisioned it. It's one thing to change your own mind about a contribution. It's much more emotionally difficult when the contribution you'll be able to make is affected by circumstances beyond your control.

As discussed earlier, people are much more comfortable when they have a sense of agency about the work they're doing. Finding things that you can control and focusing your efforts on them is one way to feel better about a change of circumstances. You'll no longer feel quite as helpless about your work life.

Finding a New Job

When you start looking for a new job after losing one, two significant issues often arise. First, you have to provide some explanation for why you're no longer working for your previous employer. Second, your search can be long and frustrating.

Unfortunately, losing a job can carry a stigma, even if the loss had nothing to do with your performance. Research on the *representativeness heuristic* demonstrates that people base their judgments about a person on what is brought to mind by that individual. Some out-of-work people were fired for poor performance or aren't working very hard to get a new job, and that stereotype influences the evaluation of people to whom it doesn't apply.

Recruiters are often unaware of this bias, but applicants find it harder to be considered seriously if they're currently out of work than if they're looking to leave one firm to join another. That's one reason people are more likely to get job offers when they're currently employed.

Because recruiters are going to make tacit assumptions about your unemployment, address why you aren't working head-on. If you have a good relationship with your previous employers, ask them to serve as a reference and reinforce your explanation about departing from your previous job. If particular weaknesses of yours contributed to your job loss, discuss what you've done to remedy them. Many prospective employers will be impressed by your willingness to overcome a failure and to improve. Those that aren't probably wouldn't have seriously considered your application anyway. A recurring theme in this book is that honesty really is the best policy in the long term when it comes to dealing with negative information about yourself.

Because your job search is likely to take time, it's important to develop a routine that keeps you focused, sharp, and upbeat. Searches are slow. You face a lot of waiting, and your habits around getting up and going to work have been disrupted. It's easy to lose motivation.

So focus on the process of the search rather than on the outcomes. Create a routine that's productive but includes enough flexibility to take phone calls and interviews as they come up. Check employment websites daily for new postings. Develop new job-related skills by taking classes in person or online and reading.

The job search can also be lonely. You no longer have a community of colleagues. Your former coworkers and members of your social network who are still employed may feel guilty about not being able to help you, putting a strain on your relationships with them. Volunteering for a local nonprofit is an excellent way to find a temporary community while you're searching for a job. Many nonprofits would benefit from having someone with your skills around—even for a short period. You may even meet people who can help your job search. Similarly, consider signing on with a temp agency. You might associate temp agencies with menial tasks, but in the modern economy, there are also many companies hiring temporary workers for highly skilled positions. That will get you into a workplace and may well connect you with people who can ultimately offer you full-time employment.

The work you do to improve your skills and to benefit other organizations through temporary or volunteer work will provide good stories in job interviews, demonstrating your resourcefulness. Employers know that your work life will have good times and bad times. It's easy to look productive when times are good. If you demonstrate that you can also be productive when times are bad, your resilience will impress recruiters.

THE TAKEAWAYS

Your Brains

Motivational Brain

- It's natural to feel grief after a career setback.
- The five stages of grief are not automatic, but they often occur after a loss.
- Shame is an outward-facing emotion, concerned with other people's reactions to something you've done.

Social Brain

- In an *upward* social comparison, you compare yourself with someone more advanced than you are; in a *downward* social comparison, you compare yourself with someone less advanced than you are.

Cognitive Brain

- *Ad hoc categories* are organized around goals, and members are rated according to their similarity to the ideal.

Your Tips

- Social comparisons are most effective when the person you compare yourself with is similar to you.

- Self-comparison is often more useful than other-comparison.

- Try not to define success too narrowly.

- Be willing to give up goals that are preventing your success or your satisfaction with your work.

- Maintain good relationships with former colleagues.

- Give yourself a chance to grieve following a job loss.

- Shame is rarely helpful in the workplace. Confront it head-on.

- Be aware that stigma can attend a job loss, even if the loss wasn't due to your own actions.

- Maintain a routine when searching for employment after a job loss.

- Volunteering or taking temp work between jobs can benefit you.

Write Your Story

C an you remember what it was like to be eight years old? Really remember? Chances are you can't. I'm sure you can look at eight-year-olds and see the things they're doing and remember some events of your life. But it's hard to truly project yourself back into the thoughts and feelings you had at that age.

I was thinking about that not long ago when I stumbled on diaries I kept as a kid (at the insistence of my mother, who said I'd want to see them in the future). I read about scores of kickball games at school, a description of a new mechanical pencil I got, and a visit to the Franklin Institute, in Philadelphia (where, apparently, I got a souvenir coin I liked so much that I traced it into my diary). Many of these details were things I had forgotten, and none of them seemed important enough to commemorate in a diary.

You lose the details not just of your childhood but of every stage of your life. A central principle of the cognitive brain is that the greater the overlap between the information in your current environment and the information that was present in the initial experience, the more likely you are to recall that experience. That's why you can remember so many details of your life that you hadn't thought about in years if you revisit a childhood home or a place you vacationed many years before. And that's why the easiest things for you to remember about your past are the ones that are most compatible with how you see the world right now. Your "now" affects your view of the past.

One result of this aspect of memory is that it can be hard to really appreciate the trajectory of your career. You'll forget about early career anxieties as you move on. You may fail to recognize the magnitude of the contributions you've made, because they've been part of your life for a while. When you find it hard to remember the details of where you started, it can be difficult to see how far you've come.

To help you track your progress, keep a record of your career. Perhaps you'll be inspired to maintain a regular diary. But even if you aren't, pick a date each year. It might be your birthday, or New Year's Day, or some other date with meaning for you. Take a little time to write about your work life that year. Write about the day-to-day tasks you do, the people you work with, your hopes, dreams, and fears. Write about things you're proud of and also the mistakes you've made. Consider saving your calendars from work as well so that you have a record of how you spent your time.

And—every once in a while—take a look back at what your "now" looked like in the past. You'll see how much your aspirations and worries change over time. Some events that you thought were going to be important will fade. Others that seemed inconsequential at the time may have proved crucial. Some goals you had earlier will remain priorities. You may also recognize that things you thought you'd never do have become a central part of what brings you satisfaction at work.

If you're lucky enough to stay healthy, your career will soak up more than 75,000 hours of your life. Yet when you ask other people about their careers, you say "What do you do?" and expect them to boil that down to a word (professor, manager, entrepreneur) or a sentence or two. Your story is richer than that—and you'd like to be able to appreciate as much of it as possible.

Bumper-sticker wisdom says that people don't lie on their deathbeds and say, "I wish I spent more time at the office." But people do take great pride in the contributions they made, the people whose lives their work touched, and the colleagues whose careers they enriched. They relish their successes and are proud of the obstacles they overcame. Even failures often become good stories when enough time has gone by.

So my advice is to write it down. Savor the details. And remember that the four saddest letters in the English language are TGIF.* If your work life is just a way to pass the time between weekends, you're missing out on a great adventure.

---

*Thank God It's Friday (which was a saying before it was a restaurant chain).

BIBLIOGRAPHY

Chapter 1

Bureau of Labor Statistics. *Jobs, Labor Market Experience, and Earnings Growth among Americans at 50: Results from a Longitudinal Survey*. Washington, DC: USDL17-1158 (2015).

Gentner, D. "Some Interesting Differences between Nouns and Verbs." *Cognition and Brain Theory* 4, no. 2 (1981): 161–178.

McCabe, D. P., and A. D. Castel. "Seeing Is Believing: The Effect of Brain Images on Judgments of Scientific Reasoning." *Cognition* 107, no. 1 (2008): 343–352.

Medin, D. L., and A. Ortony. "Psychological Essentialism." In *Similarity and Analogical Reasoning*, edited by S. Vosniadou and A. Ortony, 179–195. New York: Cambridge University Press, 1989.

Chapter 2

Bardi, A., and S. H. Schwartz. "Values and Behavior: Strength and Structure of Relations." *Personality and Social Psychology Bulletin* 29, no. 10 (2003): 1207–1220.

Chen, P., P. C. Ellsworth, and N. Schwarz. "Finding a Fit or Developing It: Implicit Theories about Achieving Passion for Work." *Personality and Social Psychology Bulletin* 41, no. 10 (2015): 1411–1424.

Dawson, J. "A History of Vocation: Tracing a Keyword of Work, Meaning, and Moral Purpose." *Adult Education Quarterly* 55, no. 3 (2005): 220–231.

Dik, B. J., and R. D. Duffy. "Calling and Vocation at Work." *The Counseling Psychologist* 37, no. 3 (2009): 424–450.

Duffy, R. D., B. J. Dik, and M. F. Steger. "Calling and Work-related Outcomes: Commitment as a Mediator." *Journal of Vocational Behavior* 78 (2011): 210–218.

Gilovich, T., and V. H. Medvec. "The Temporal Pattern to the Experience of Regret." *Journal of Personality and Social Psychology* 67, no. 3 (1994): 357–365.

Harter, J. K., F. L. Schmidt, and C. L. Keyes. "Well-being in the Workplace and Its Relationship to Business Outcomes: A Review of the Gallup Studies." In *Flourishing: The Positive Person and the Good Life*, edited by C. L. Keyes and J. Haidt. Washington, DC: American Psychological Association, 2002.

Langer, E. J. "The Illusion of Control." *Journal of Personality and Social Psychology* 32, no. 2 (1975): 311–328.

Ward, T. B. "What's Old about New Ideas." In *The Creative Cognition Approach*, edited by S. M. Smith, T. B. Ward, and R. A. Finke, 157–178. Cambridge, MA: The MIT Press, 1995.

Chapter 3

Alter, A. L., and D. M. Oppenheimer. "Uniting the Tribes of Fluency to Form a Metacognitive Nation." *Personality and Social Psychology Review* 13, no. 3 (2009): 219–235.

Ambady, N., F. J. Bernieri, and J. A. Richeson. "Toward a Histology of Social Behavior: Judgmental Accuracy from Thin Slices of the Behavioral Stream." *Advances in Experimental Social Psychology* 32 (2000): 201–271.

Beilock, S. L. *Choke: What the Secrets of the Brain Reveal about Getting It Right When You Have To*. New York: Free Press, 2010.

Darke, S. "Anxiety and Working Memory Capacity." *Cognition and Emotion* 2, no. 2 (1987): 145–154.

Higgins, E. T., G. A. King, and G. H. Mavin. "Individual Construct Accessibility and Subjective Impressions and Recall." *Journal of Personality and Social Psychology* 43, no. 1 (1982): 35–47.

Johnson, J. H., and I. G. Sarason. "Life Stress, Depression and Anxiety: Internal-External Control as a Moderator Variable." *Journal of Psychosomatic Research* 22, no. 3 (1978): 205–208.

Nisbett, R. E., and T. D. Wilson. "The Halo Effect: Evidence for Unconscious Alteration of Judgments." *Journal of Personality and Social Psychology* 35, no. 4 (1977): 250–256.

Pickering, M. J., and S. Garrod. "Toward a Mechanistic Psychology of Dialogue." *Behavioral and Brain Sciences* 27, no. 2 (2004): 169–226.

Shafir, E. "Choosing versus Rejecting: Why Some Options Are Both Better and Worse Than Others." *Memory and Cognition* 21, no. 4 (1993): 546–556.

Shafir, E., I. Simonson, and A. Tversky. "Reason-Based Choice." *Cognition* 49 (1993): 11–36.

Spector, P. E. "Behavior in Organizations as a Function of Employee's Locus of Control." *Psychological Bulletin* 91, no. 3 (1982): 482–497.

Thompson, S. D., and H. H. Kelley. "Judgments of Responsibility for Activities in Close Relationships." *Journal of Personality and Social Psychology* 41, no. 3 (1981): 469–477.

Weaver, K., S. M. Garcia, and N. Schwarz. "The Presenter's Paradox." *Journal of Consumer Research* 39 (2012): 445–460.

Chapter 4

Gentner, D., and A. B. Markman. "Structure Mapping in Analogy and Similarity." *American Psychologist* 52, no. 1 (1997): 45–56.

Hsee, C. K. "The Evaluability Hypothesis: An Explanation of Preference Reversals for Joint and Separate Evaluation of Alternatives." *Organizational Behavior and Human Decision Processes*, 67, no. 3 (1996): 247–257.

Kruglanski, A. W., and D. M. Webster. "Motivated Closing of the Mind: 'Seizing' and 'Freezing.'" *Psychological Review* 103, no. 2 (1996): 263–283.

Kunda, Z. "The Case for Motivated Reasoning." *Psychological Bulletin* 108, no. 3 (1990): 480–498.

Lakoff, G., and M. Johnson. *Metaphors We Live By*. Chicago, IL: The University of Chicago Press, 1980.

Loschelder, D. D., M. Friese, M. Schaerer, and A. D. Galinsky. "The Too-Much-Precision Effect: When and Why Precise Anchors Backfire with Experts." *Psychological Science* 27, no. 12 (2016): 1573–1587.

Markman, A. B., and D. L. Medin. "Similarity and Alignment in Choice." *Organizational Behavior and Human Decision Processes* 63, no. 2 (1995): 117–130.

Roseman, I. J. "Appraisal Determinants of Emotions: Constructing an Accurate and Comprehensive Theory." *Cognition and Emotion* 10, no. 3 (1996): 241–278.

Russo, E. J., V. H. Medvec, and M. G. Meloy. "The Distortion of Information during Decisions." *Organizational Behavior and Human Decision Processes* 66 (1996): 102–110.

Schaerer, M., R. I. Swaab, and A. D. Galinsky. "Anchors Weigh More Than Power: Why Absolute Powerlessness Liberates Negotiators to Achieve Better Outcomes." *Psychological Science* 26, no. 2 (2015): 170–181.

Shafir, E., I. Simonson, and A. Tversky. "Reason-Based Choice." *Cognition* 49 (1993): 11–36.

Stanovich, K. E., and R. F. West. "Individual Differences in Rational Thought." *Journal of Experimental Psychology: General* 127, no. 2 (1998): 161–188.

Trope, Y., and N. Liberman. "Temporal Construal." *Psychological Review* 110, no. 3 (2003): 403–421.

Tversky, A., and D. Kahneman. "Judgment under Uncertainty: Heuristics and Biases." *Science* 185 (1974): 1124–1131.

Wilson, T. D., and J. W. Schooler. "Thinking Too Much: Introspection Can Reduce the Quality of Preferences and Decisions." *Journal of Personality and Social Psychology* 60, no. 2 (1991): 181–192.

Chapter 5

Aarts, H., P. M. Gollwitzer, and R. R. Hassin. "Goal Contagion: Perceiving Is for Pursuing." *Journal of Personality and Social Psychology* 87, no. 1 (2004): 23–37.

Basalla, G. *The Evolution of Technology*. Cambridge, UK: Cambridge University Press, 1988.

Chi, M. T. H., and K. A. VanLehn. "The Content of Physics Self-Explanations." *Journal of the Learning Sciences* 1, no. 1 (1991): 69–105.

Dunning, D., and J. Kruger. "Unskilled and Unaware of It: How Difficulties in Recognizing One's Own Incompetence Lead to Inflated Self-Assessments." *Journal of Personality and Social Psychology* 77, no. 6 (1999): 1121–1134.

Kolligian, J., and R. J. Sternberg. "Perceived Fraudulence in Young Adults: Is There an 'Imposter Syndrome'?" *Journal of Personality Assessment* 56, no. 2 (1991): 308–326.

Markman, A. B. *Knowledge Representation*. Mahwah, NJ: Lawrence Erlbaum Associates, 1999.

Markman, A. *Habits of Leadership*. New York: Perigee Books, 2013.

Markman, A. *Smart Thinking*. New York: Perigee Books, 2012.

Maxwell, N. L., and J. S. Lopus. "The Lake Wobegon Effect in Student Self-Reported Data." *American Economic Review* 84, no. 2 (1994): 201–205.

Metcalfe, J., and A. P. Shimamura, eds. *Metacognition: Knowing about Knowing*. Cambridge, MA: The MIT Press, 1994.

Roediger, H. L., and K. B. McDermott. Creating False Memories: Remembering Words Not Presented in Lists." *Journal of Experimental Psychology: Learning, Memory, and Cognition* 21, no. 4 (1995): 803–814.

Rosenblit, L., and F. C. Keil. "The Misunderstood Limits of Folk Science: An Illusion of Explanatory Depth." *Cognitive Science* 26 (2002): 521–562.

Sturgis, P., C. Roberts, and P. Smith. "Middle Alternatives Revisited: How the Neither/Nor Response Acts as a Way of Saying 'I Don't Know.'" *Sociological Methods and Research* 43, no. 1 (2014): 15–38.

Chapter 6

Brummelman, E., S. Thomaes, and C. Sedikides. "Separating Narcissism from Self-esteem." *Current Directions in Psychological Science* 25, no. 1 (2016): 8–13.

Clark, H. H. *Using Language*. New York: Cambridge University Press, 1996.

Garrod, S., and G. Doherty. "Conversation, Co-ordination and Convention: An Empirical Investigation of How Groups Establish Linguistic Conventions." *Cognition* 53 (1994): 181–215.

Keating, E., and S. L. Jarvenpaa. *Words Matter: Communicating Effectively in the New Global Office*. Oakland, CA: University of California Press, 2016.

Levelt, W. J. M. *Speaking: From Intention to Articulation*. Cambridge, MA: The MIT Press, 1989.

Levinson, S. C. "Deixis." In *Handbook of Pragmatics*, edited by L. R. Horn and G. Ward, 97–121. Malden, MA: Blackwell Publishing Ltd, 2004.

McTighe, J., and R. S. Thomas. "Backward Design for Forward Action." *Educational Leadership* 60, no. 5 (2003): 52–55.

Chapter 7

Anderson, M. C., and B. A. Spellman. "On the Status of Inhibitory Mechanisms in Cognition: Memory Retrieval as a Model Case." *Psychological Review* 102, no. 1 (1995): 68–100.

Anderson, M. C., C. Green, and K. C. McCulloch. "Similarity and Inhibition in Long-term Memory: Evidence for a Two-Factor Theory." *Journal of Experimental Psychology: Learning, Memory, and Cognition* 26, no. 5 (2000): 1141–1159.

Dalston, B. H., and D. G. Behm. "Effects of Noise and Music on Human and Task Performance: A Systematic Review." *Occupational Ergonomics* 7 (2007): 143–152.

Dobbs, S., A. Furnham, and A. McClelland. "The Effect of Background Music and Noise on the Cognitive Test Performance of Introverts and Extraverts." *Applied Cognitive Psychology* 25 (2011): 307–313.

Drucker, P. F. *The Practice of Management*. New York: HarperCollins Publishers, 1954.

Emberson, L. L., G. Lupyan, M. H. Goldstein, and M. J. Spivey. "Overheard Cell-Phone Conversations: When Less Speech Is More Distracting." *Psychological Science* 21, no. 20 (2010): 1383–1388.

Fiske, A. P. "The Four Elementary Forms of Sociality: Framework for a Unified Theory of Social Relations." *Psychological Review* 99 (1992): 689–723.

Hanczakowski, M., C. P. Beaman, and D. M. Jones. "Learning through Clamor: The Allocation and Perception of Study Time in Noise." *Journal of Experimental Psychology: General* 147, no. 7 (2018): 1005–1022.

Hildreth, J. A. D. and C. Anderson. "Failure at the Top: How Power Undermines Collaborative Performance." *Journal of Personality and Social Psychology* 110, no. 2 (2016): 261–286.

Hillman, C. H., K. I. Erickson, and A. F. Kramer. "Be Smart, Exercise Your Heart: Exercise Effects on Brain and Cognition." *Nature Reviews Neuroscience* 9 (2008): 58–65.

Hofstede, G., G. J. Hofstede, and M. Minkov. *Cultures and Organizations* (3rd ed.). New York: McGraw-Hill, 2010.

Humphreys, M. S., and W. Revelle. "Personality, Motivation, and Performance: A Theory of the Relationship between Individual Differences and Information Processing." *Psychological Review* 91, no. 2 (1984): 153–184.

Jonason, P. K., S. Slomski, and J. Partyka. "The Dark Triad at Work: How Toxic Employees Get Their Way." *Personality and Individual Differences* 52, no. 3 (2012): 449–453.

Mednick, S. C., D. J. Cai, J. Kanady, and S. P. A. Drummond. "Comparing the Benefits of Caffeine, Naps, and Placebo on Verbal, Motor, and Perceptual Memory." *Behavioural Brain Research* 193 (2008): 79–86.

Pashler, H. E. *The Psychology of Attention.* Cambridge, MA: The MIT Press, 1998.

Paulhus, D. L., and K. M. Williams. "The Dark Triad of Personality: Narcissism, Machiavellianism, and Psychopathy." *Journal of Research in Personality* 36, no. 6 (2002): 556–563.

Scullin, M. K., and D. L. Bliwise. "Sleep, Cognition, and Normal Aging: Integrating a Half-century of Multidisciplinary Research." *Perspectives on Psychological Science* 10, no. 1 (2015): 97–137.

Tannenbaum, S. I., and C. P. Cerasoli. "Do Team and Individual Debriefs Enhance Performance?" *Human Factors* 55, no. 1 (2013): 231–245.

Walker, M. P. "The Role of Sleep in Cognition and Emotion." *Annals of the New York Academy of Sciences* 1156 (2009): 168–197.

Walker, M. P., and R. Stickgold. "Sleep, Memory, and Plasticity." *Annual Review of Psychology* 57 (2006): 139–166.

Yerkes, R. M., and J. D. Dodson. "The Relation of Strength of Stimulus to Rapidity of Habit-Formation." *Journal of Comparative Neurology and Psychology* 18 (1908): 459–482.

Chapter 8

Arkes, H. R., and C. Blumer. "The Psychology of Sunk Cost." *Organizational Behavior and Human Decision Processes* 35 (1985): 124–140.

Boland-Prom, K., and S. C. Anderson. "Teaching Ethical Decision Making Using Dual Relationship Principles as a Case Example." *Journal of Social Work Education* 41, no. 3 (2005): 495–510.

Brehm, J. W., and E. A. Self. "The Intensity of Motivation." *Annual Review of Psychology* 40 (1989): 109–131.

Cooper, V. W. "Homophily or the Queen Bee Syndrome: Female Evaluation of Female Leadership." *Small Group Research* 28, no. 4 (1997): 483–499.

Duckworth, A. L., C. Peterson, M. D. Matthews, and D. R. Kelly. "Grit: Perseverance and Passion for Long-term Goals." *Psychological Review* 92, no. 6 (2007): 1087–1101.

Eagly, A. H., and J. L. Chin. "Diversity and Leadership in a Changing World." *American Psychologist* 65, no. 3 (2010): 216–224.

Gigerenzer, G. "Why the Distinction between Single-Event Probabilities and Frequencies Is Important for Psychology (and Vice Versa)." In *Subjective Probability*, edited by G. Wright and P. Ayton, 129–161. New York: John Wiley and Sons, 1994.

Gigerenzer, G. *Adaptive Thinking: Rationality in the Real World.* New York: Oxford University Press, 2000.

Johnson, H. M., and C. M. Seifert. "Sources of the Continued Influence Effect: When Misinformation in Memory Affects Later Instances." *Journal of Experimental Psychology: Learning, Memory, and Cognition* 20, no. 6 (1994): 1420–1436.

Lazonick, W., and M. O'Sullivan. "Maximizing Shareholder Value: A New Ideology for Corporate Governance." *Economy and Society* 1 (2000): 13–35.

Leung, A. K., W. W. Maddux, A. D. Galinsky, and C. Y. Chiu. "Multicultural Experience Enhances Creativity: The When and How." *American Psychologist* 63, no. 3 (2008): 169–181.

Lucas, H. C., and J. M. Goh. "Disruptive Technology: How Kodak Missed the Digital Photography Revolution." *Journal of Strategic Information Systems* 18, no. 1 (2009): 46–55.

Markman, A. *Smart Change: Five Tools to Create New and Sustainable Habits in Yourself and Others.* New York: Perigee Books, 2014.

Mavin, S. "Queen Bees, Wannabees, and Afraid to Bees: No More 'Best Enemies' for Women in Management." *British Journal of Management* 19 (2008): S75–S84.

McFadden, K. L., and E. R. Towell. "Aviation Human Factors: A Framework for the New Millennium." *Journal of Air Transport Management* 5, no. 4 (1999): 177–184.

Mischel, W., and Y. Shoda. "A Cognitive-Affective System Theory of Personality: Reconceptualizing Situations, Dispositions, Dynamics, and Invariance in Personality Structure." *Psychological Review* 102, no. 2 (1995): 246–268.

Nisbett, R. E., ed. *Rules for Reasoning.* Hillsdale, NJ: Lawrence Erlbaum Associates, 1993.

Oettingen, G. *Rethinking Positive Thinking: Inside the New Science of Motivation.* New York: Current, 2014.

Ross, L. D. "The Intuitive Psychologist and His Shortcomings: Distortions in the Attribution Process." In *Advances in Experimental Social Psychology*, Vol. 10, edited by L. Berkowitz. New York: Academic Press, 1977.

Spetzler, C., H. Winter, and J. Meyer. *Decision Quality.* New York: Wiley, 2016.

Thorsteinsson, E. B., and J. E. James. "A Meta-analysis of the Effects of Experimental Manipulations of Social Support during Laboratory Stress." *Psychology and Health* 14 (1999): 869–886.

Tversky, A., and D. Kahneman. "Judgment under Uncertainty: Heuristics and Biases." *Science* 185 (1974): 1124–1131.

Vergauwe, J., B. Wille, J. Hofmans, R. B. Kaiser, and F. De Fruyt. "The Double-Edged Sword of Leader Charisma: Understanding the Curvilinear Relationship between Charismatic Personality and Leader Effectiveness." *Journal of Personality and Social Psychology* 114, no. 1 (2018): 110–130.

Weathersby, G. B. "Leadership vs. Management." *Management Review* 88, no. 3 (1999): 5.

Wollitzky-Taylor, K. B., J. D. Horowitz, M. B. Powers, and M. J. Telch. "Psychological Approaches in the Treatment of Specific Phobias: A Meta-analysis." *Clinical Psychology Review* 28, no. 6 (2008): 1021–1037.

Woodruff, P. *The Ajax Dilemma: Justice, Fairness, and Rewards.* New York: Oxford University Press, 2011.

Chapter 9

Ajzen, I., and M. Fishbein. "Attitude-Behavior Relations: A Theoretical Analysis and Review of Empirical Research." *Psychological Bulletin* 84, no. 5 (1977): 888–918.

Artz, B., A. H. Goodall, and A. J. Oswald. "Boss Competence and Worker Well-being." *Industrial and Labor Relations Review* 70, no. 2 (2017): 419–450.

Brickman, P., and D. T. Campbell. "Hedonic Relativism and Planning the Good Society." In *Adaptation Level Theory: A Symposium*, edited by M. H. Appley, 287–302. New York: Academic Press, 1971.

Campbell, C. R., and M. J. Martinko. "An Integrative Attributional Perspective of Empowerment and Learned Helplessness: A Multimethod Field Study." *Journal of Management* 24, no. 2 (1998): 173–200.

Dane, E., and B. J. Brummel. "Examining Workplace Mindfulness and Its Relation to Job Performance and Turnover Intention." *Human Relations* 67, no. 1 (2014): 105–128.

de Bloom, J., S. A. E. Geurts, S. Sonnentag, T. Taris, C. de Weerth, and M. A. Kompier. "How Does a Vacation from Work Affect Employee Health and Well-being?" *Psychology and Health* 26, no. 12 (2011): 1606–1622.

de Bloom, J., S. A. Geurts, and M. A. Kompier. "Vacation (After-) Effects on Employee Health and Well-being, and the Role of Vacation Activities, Experiences, and Sleep." *Journal of Happiness Studies* 14, no. 2 (2013): 613–633.

Fritz, C., A. M. Ellis, C. A. Demsky, B. C. Lin, and F. Guros. "Embracing Work Breaks: Recovering from Work Stress." *Organizational Dynamics* 42 (2013): 274–280.

Gensowsky, M. "Personality, IQ, and Lifetime Earnings." *Labour Economics* 51 (2018): 170–183.

Gilbert, D. T., and T. D. Wilson. "Miswanting: Some Problems in the Forecasting of Future Affective States." In *Thinking and Feeling: The Role of Affect in Social Cognition*, edited by J. Forgas, 178–197. New York: Cambridge University Press, 2000.

Gilbert, D. T., M. J. Gill, and T. D. Wilson. "The Future Is Now: Temporal Correction in Affective Forecasting." *Organizational Behavior and Human Decision Processing* 88, no. 1 (2002): 430–444.

Holyoak, K. J., and D. Simon. "Bidirectional Reasoning in Decision Making." *Journal of Experimental Psychology: General* 128, no. 1 (1999): 3–31.

Jackson, D., A. Firtko, and M. Edenborough. "Personal Resilience as a Strategy for Surviving and Thriving in the Face of Workplace Adversity: A Literature Review." *Journal of Advanced Nursing* 60, no. 1 (2007): 1–9.

Judge, T. A., B. A. Livingston, and C. Hurst. "Do Nice Guys—and Gals—Really Finish Last? The Joint Effects of Sex and Agreeableness on Income." *Journal of Personality and Social Psychology* 102, no. 2 (2012): 390–407.

Koo, M., and A. Fishbach. "Climbing the Goal Ladder: How Upcoming Actions Increase Level of Aspiration." *Journal of Personality and Social Psychology* 90, no. 1 (2010): 1–13.

Markman, A. B., and D. L. Medin. "Similarity and Alignment in Choice." *Organizational Behavior and Human Decision Processes* 63, no. 2 (1995): 117–130.

McDonald, D. *The Golden Passport: Harvard Business School and the Limits of Capitalism, and the Moral Failure of the MBA Elite*. New York: Harper Business, 2017.

Miller, K. I., B. H. Ellis, E. G. Zook, and J. S. Lyles. "An Integrated Model of Communication, Stress, and Burnout in the Workplace." *Communication Research* 17, no. 3 (1990): 300–326.

Ovsiankina, M. "Die Wiederafunahme unterbrochener Handlungen" ["The Resumption of Interrupted Tasks"]. *Psychologische Forschung* 11 (1928): 302–379.

Russo, E. J., V. H. Medvec, and M. G. Meloy. "The Distortion of Information during Decisions." *Organizational Behavior and Human Decision Processes* 66 (1996): 102–110.

Zeigarnik, B. "Das Behalten erledigter unt unerledigter Handlungen ["The Retention of Completed and Uncompleted Actions"]. *Psychologische Forschung* 9 (1927): 1–85.

Zhang, S., and A. B. Markman. "Overcoming the Early Entrant Advantage: The Role of Alignable and Nonalignable Differences." *Journal of Marketing Research* 35 (1998): 413–426.

Chapter 10

Ashton, W. A., and A. Fuehrer. "Effects of Gender and Gender Role Identification of Participant and Type of Social Support Resource on Support Seeking." *Sex Roles* 7–8 (1993): 461–476.

Barsalou, L. W. "Ad hoc Categories." *Memory and Cognition* 11 (1983): 211–227.

Barsalou, L. W. "Ideals, Central Tendency and Frequency of Instantiation as Determinants of Graded Structure in Categories." *Journal of Experimental Psychology: Learning, Memory and Cognition* 11, no. 4 (1985): 629–654.

Bengtsson, M., and S. Kock. "'Coopetition' in Business Networks—To Cooperate and Compete Simultaneously." *Industrial Marketing Management* 29, no. 5 (2000): 411–426.

Blau, D. M., and P. K. Robins. "Job Search Outcomes for the Employed and Unemployed." *Journal of Political Economy* 98, no. 3 (1990): 637–655.

Chun, J. S., J. Brockner, and D. De Cremer. "How Temporal and Social Comparisons in Performance Evaluation Affect Fairness Perceptions." *Organizational Behavior and Human Decision Processes* 145, no. 1 (2018): 1–15.

Cohen, T. R., S. T. Wolf, A. T. Panter, and C. A. Insko. "Introducing the GASP Scale: A Measure of Guilt and Shame Proneness." *Journal of Personality and Social Psychology* 100, no. 5 (2011): 947–966.

Kübler-Ross, E. *On Death and Dying.* New York: Scribner and Sons, 1969.

McKee-Ryan, F., Z. Song, C. R. Wanberg, and A. J. Kinicki. "Psychological and Physical Well-being during Unemployment." *Journal of Applied Psychology* 90, no. 1 (2005): 53–76.

Neff, K. "Self-compassion: An Alternative Conceptualization of a Healthy Attitude toward Oneself." *Self and Identity* 2, no. 2 (2003): 85–101.

Nisbett, R. E., and T. D. Wilson. "The Halo Effect: Evidence for Unconscious Alteration of Judgments." *Journal of Personality and Social Psychology* 35, no. 4 (1977): 250–256.

Oettingen, G., H.-j. Pak, and K. Schnetter. "Self-regulation of Goal-setting: Turning Free Fantasies about the Future into Binding Goals." *Journal of Personality and Social Psychology* 80, no. 5 (2001): 736–753.

Pennebaker, J. W. "Writing about Emotional Experiences as a Therapeutic Process." *Psychological Science* 8, no. 3 (1997): 162–166.

Scher, S. J., and J. M. Darley. "How Effective Are the Things People Say to Apologize? Effects of the Realization of the Apology Speech Act." *Journal of Psycholinguistic Research* 26, no. 1 (1997): 127–140.

Shipp, A. J., S. Furst-Holloway, T. B. Harris, and B. Rosen. "Gone Today but Here Tomorrow: Extending the Unfolding Model of Turnover to Consider Boomerang Employees." *Personnel Psychology* 67 (2014): 421–462.

Smith, R. H., E. Diener, and D. H. Wedell. "Intrapersonal and Social Comparison Determinants of Happiness: A Range-frequency Analysis." *Journal of Personality and Social Psychology* 56, no. 3 (1989): 317–325.

Tversky, A., and D. Kahneman. "Judgment under Uncertainty: Heuristics and Biases." *Science* 185 (1974): 1124–1131.

Woolley, K., and A. Fishbach. "For the Fun of It: Harnessing Immediate Rewards to Increase Persistence in Long-term Goals." *Journal of Consumer Research* 42, no. 6 (2016): 952–966.

Epilogue

Tulving, E., and D. M. Thomson. "Encoding Specificity and Retrieval Processes in Episodic Memory." *Psychological Review* 80 (1973): 352–373.

INDEX

ACKNOWLEDGMENTS

The front cover of a book like this names one person as the author, making it hard to know that a large number of people are truly responsible for its existence.

This book would never have come into being without Kate Davis and Rich Bellis at Fast Company and Sarah Green Carmichael and Amy Gallo at HBR, who spent the past several years suggesting so many workplace-related stories that I was inspired to address these issues in a book. I've enjoyed working with them immensely and hope to continue to do so in the future.

A huge thank-you to the many many many (many) people on social media who responded to my repeated requests for stories about aspects of their careers. People were quite generous in sharing their experiences. I apologize that I wasn't able to use every story they sent in.

As always, my deep appreciation goes to my amazing agent, Giles Anderson, who pushes me to keep writing and navigates the publishing world expertly so that I don't have to.

My work with the Human Dimensions of Organizations program at the University of Texas has informed a lot of my perspective on careers. Thanks to Amy Ware, Lewis Miller, Lauren Lief, Jessica Crawford, Rolee Rios, and Alyx Dykema for their hard work on behalf of the program. This book is dedicated to them. Thanks also to Randy Diehl, Marc Musick, Richard Flores, Esther Raizen, and the entire dean's office in the College of Liberal Arts at UT for supporting the program over the years. My deepest appreciation to the faculty and students of the program for sharing their wisdom.

During the evolution of this book, people volunteered to give me feedback on the manuscript. Thanks to Vera Hinojosa, Elizabeth Molitor, and Lara Reichle for taking the time to read it—typos and all. And thanks to my *Two Guys on Your Head* partner in crime, Bob Duke, for discussions and comments on my writing. And Heidi Grant and David Burkus provided interesting perspectives along the way.

The folks at Harvard Business Review Press were instrumental in making this book a reality. I appreciate the willingness of Jeff Kehoe to take on this project; his feedback, along with that of the reviewers (including Kate Davis and Pete Foley), improved the book greatly. I love the cover design by Stephani Finks and her team, and the clean look of the inside of the book that the text design team put together. The marketing team spearheaded by Julie Devoll has done a fantastic job getting this book out in front of people.

Finally, my love and thanks to Leora Orent for listening to me talk about this project endlessly and to Lucas, 'Eylam, and Niv for providing a visceral reminder of what an early career looks like. Some of their stories also found their way into the book. Thanks also to my parents, Sondra and Ed Markman, whose careers and advice affected my decisions about how to navigate my own career. And thanks for making me keep that diary in grade school, Mom.

ABOUT THE AUTHOR

ART MARKMAN earned his ScB in Cognitive Science from Brown University and his MA and PhD in Psychology from the University of Illinois. He taught at Northwestern University and Columbia University before joining the faculty at the University of Texas at Austin in 1998, where he is now the Annabel Irion Worsham Centennial Professor of Psychology and Marketing as well as director of the IC^2 Institute. He was the founding director of the university's program in the Human Dimensions of Organizations, an innovative program that uses the humanities and the social and behavioral sciences to teach people in business, government, nonprofits, and the military about people. Markman has written over 150 scholarly papers on research projects focusing on topics in higher-level thinking, including reasoning, decision making, and motivation. He served as executive editor of the journal *Cognitive Science* for nine years. Markman is committed to bringing insights from cognitive science to a broader audience. He blogs regularly for *Psychology Today, Fast Company*, and *Harvard Business Review*, and he has a radio show and podcast called *Two Guys on Your Head*. He is the author of several books, including *Smart Thinking, Smart Change, Habits of Leadership*, and *Brain Briefs*. When he isn't working or spending time with his family he can be found playing the saxophone in a ska band.